Design and the modern magazine

MANCHESTER
1824

Manchester University Press

STUDIES IN
DESIGN

general editor:
Christopher Breward

founding editor:
Paul Greenhalgh

Design and the modern magazine

edited by
Jeremy Aynsley and Kate Forde

WITHDRAWN

Manchester University Press
Manchester and New York

distributed exclusively in the USA by Palgrave

Copyright © Manchester University Press 2007

While copyright in the volume as a whole is vested in Manchester University Press, copyright in individual chapters belongs to their respective authors, and no chapter may be reproduced wholly or in part without the express permission in writing of both author and publisher.

Published by Manchester University Press
Oxford Road, Manchester M13 9NR, UK
and Room 400, 175 Fifth Avenue, New York, NY 10010, USA
www.manchesteruniversitypress.co.uk

Distributed exclusively in the USA by
Palgrave, 175 Fifth Avenue, New York,
NY 10010, USA

Distributed exclusively in Canada by
UBC Press, University of British Columbia, 2029 West Mall,
Vancouver, BC, Canada V6T 1Z2

British Library Cataloguing-in-Publication Data
A catalogue record for this book is available from the British Library

Library of Congress Cataloging-in-Publication Data applied for

ISBN   0 7190 7549 1 *hardback*
EAN   978 0 7190 7549 0

First published 2007

16 15 14 13 12 11 10 09 08 07   10 9 8 7 6 5 4 3 2 1

Typeset in ITC Giovanni
by Carnegie Publishing, Lancaster
Printed in Great Britain
by CPI, Bath

Contents

STUDIES IN DESIGN anthologies

General editor's foreword

When the Manchester University Press series 'Studies in Design' was launched under the editorship of Paul Greenhalgh in 1990, its aim was to provide a space for the dissemination of research that was developing internationally in the new field of the history and theory of design and material culture, setting design in all its forms within a wider intellectual framework. More than fifteen years later, the series has demonstrated its commitment to this mission through the publication of an expanding list of monographs and edited collections by established and younger scholars whose work has made a real impact on the development of the discipline. A major strength of the series has been its close relationship, through the professional backgrounds of its authors, to the teaching of design history in universities and colleges, in departments of history, cultural studies, art history and design. It seems fitting then that the sub-series 'Studies in Design Anthologies', of which this is the second publication, offers a format in which the work of graduates who have benefited from the development of the scholarship noted above can find a broader circulation.

The postgraduate programme in the History of Design, founded in 1983 and run by the Royal College of Art and the Victoria & Albert Museum, has also played a pioneering role in defining the territory and direction of design historical research in an international context. It has produced generations of students who have gone on to produce influential work in the worlds of education, museums and galleries, retail, design consultancy and journalism. Several have completed publications in the Studies in Design series. The Studies in Design Anthologies offer a valuable insight into the original work that this community has engaged with. Their chapters have been sourced from the extensive archive of the V&A/RCA programme and selected on the grounds of their scholarly and innovative qualities. Each volume has been edited by prominent scholars associated with the programme, and through its introductory essay and range of case studies aims to provide a variety of themed approaches to the study of objects as powerful mediators of design, production and consumption in particular fields.

This anthology focuses on the modern magazine, a category that has, surprisingly, been relatively overlooked in the broader design historical literature. Its chapters suggest a range of sources and methods which might be applied to this most ephemeral of subjects, and shows how the content and appearance of the magazine can be mobilised in wider discussions of Modernism and modernity, consumer society and culture and technology. Like other titles in the series it demonstrates the ongoing development and health of the discipline and offers a unique insight into the uses of design historical approaches as a means of unpacking the material nature of the past.

Christopher Breward

List of figures

List of contributors

Jeremy Aynsley is Professor of Design History at the Royal College of Art where he is also Head of the School of Humanities. He studied History of Art at the University of Sussex (BA, MA) before completing a PhD (RCA) on the subject of early twentieth-century graphic design in Germany. Jeremy Aynsley taught Design History at a number of institutions and was Senior Lecturer at Brighton University before joining the V&A/RCA History of Design in 1991 as Course Tutor. Since 2001, he has been Director of the AHRC Centre for the Study of the Domestic Interior, a research centre run in conjunction with Royal Holloway University of London and the Victoria and Albert Museum.

Marie-Louise Bowallius is a lecturer in Design History, specialising in graphic design. She is engaged in a research project entitled 'Swedish Design and National Identity in Historical and International Perspectives'. She graduated from the V&A/RCA History of Design programme in 1999.

Emma Ferry studied History at the University of Southampton and was later awarded the Oliver Ford Scholarship to study History of Design at the Victoria and Albert Museum and the Royal College of Art (1995–97). Having worked at Southampton Art Gallery and for the National Trust, she currently lectures at the School of Art and Design History at Kingston University. She has recently been awarded her PhD for research carried out on Macmillan's 'Art at Home' series.

Kate Forde is Assistant Curator at the Wellcome Trust. She graduated from the RCA/V&A History of Design MA course in 2001.

Ken Garland became the Art Editor of *Design* magazine from 1956 to 1962, after completing his studies in graphic design at the Central School of Arts and Crafts, London. He left to establish his own graphic design studio, Ken Garland and Associates, where his clients included Galt Toys, Race Furniture, William Heinemann, Paramount Pictures, The Science Museum, Cambridge University

Press, The Ministry of Technology and The Arts Council. He has published widely on the subject of design and has taught at various institutions including the Royal College of Art, the Central School of Art and Design and the National College of Art and Design, Dublin. He lectures internationally and is currently Visiting Professor in Information Design at the Universidad de las Americas, Puebla, Mexico, and Visiting Professor at Brighton University, UK.

Trevor Keeble is Head of the School of Art and Design History at Kingston University. He graduated with a BA (Hons) in Interior Architecture from Brighton University in 1994. He completed the V&A/RCA MA History of Design course in 1997 having written a dissertation entitled 'Everyday Wrappings. A Mediated Message of Domestic Design Reform: Woman Magazine 1952–1956'. He success-fully completed his PhD thesis entitled 'The Domestic Moment: Design, Taste and Identity in the Late Victorian Interior' in the History of Design Department at the RCA in 2005.

Victoria Kelley studied Modern History at Oxford University (1986–89) and received her MA from the V&A/RCA History of Design programme in 1995. She currently teaches at Kent Institute of Art and Design and is studying for a PhD at the Royal College of Art.

Emily King graduated from the V&A/RCA MA History of Design in 1993 and obtained her PhD from Kingston University with a thesis on the design of type between 1987 and 1997. She lectures and writes widely and has been the design editor of *Frieze* magazine since 2000. Her most recent book, *Movie Posters* was published by Mitchell Beazley in 2003.

Gillian Naylor, MA, PhD, helped set up the V&A/RCA MA course when it was first launched in 1981. After reading French at Somerville College, Oxford, she joined the staff of *Design* magazine and subsequently taught history of design and architecture courses at Brighton and Kingston Polytechnics, before moving to the RCA in 1980. She was a member of the CNAA History of Art and Design Panel, a founder member of the Design History Society, and a committee member of the Decorative Art Society. She is now an Honorary Fellow of the Royal College of Art, a Patron of the Design History Society, and in 2003 was granted an honorary doctorate of design for exceptional achievement from Kingston University. She has published numerous books, articles and papers relating to nineteenth- and twentieth-century design history, and has lectured internationally.

Linda Sandino graduated from the V&A/RCA History of Design MA programme in 1991 and is at present working as an oral historian for the National Life Story Collection at the British Library interviewing artists, craftspeople and designers for the National Sound Archive. She was formerly Associate Research Coordina-tor at Camberwell College of Arts and has taught at various colleges including Central St Martins College of Art and Design and the Royal College of Art. Her most recent publication is 'Studio Jewellery: Mapping the Absent Body' in *The*

Persistence of Craft, edited by Paul Greenhalgh (London and Brunswick, NJ: Rutgers University, 2002).

Zoé Nicole Whitley is Assistant Curator of Prints and Contemporary Works in the Word and Image Department of the Victoria & Albert Museum, London. She graduated from the V&A/RCA History of Design MA programme in 2003.

Acknowledgements

The editors would like to thank all staff and students on the V&A/RCA History of Design course who have contributed to the stimulating academic context in which much of the research towards this publication developed. In particular, Penny Sparke and Susie McKellar undertook the initial discussion to launch the series. Staff in many libraries around the United Kingdom helped individual research, and in particular we are grateful to staff at the National Art Library at the Victoria and Albert Museum and the Library of the Royal College of Art. Preparation of the book was assisted by a grant awarded by the Research Committee of the Royal College of Art.

Introduction

Jeremy Aynsley and Kate Forde

Definitions and aims

In recent years, the modern magazine, the subject of this book, has been the focus of a variety of interpretations from within cultural and historical studies. A product of mass circulation, the magazine preceded radio and television as an affordable source of knowledge and entertainment, bringing a wide range of issues to a broad population. Even though not all members of the public were in a position to purchase their own personal copy, its very means of circulation, often through handing down and other kinds of informal dispersal, meant that the magazine became a ubiquitous object that played a central part in the flow of modern life and people's social and cultural identities. To the design historian, the magazine presents a number of challenges of interpretation and understanding. Its distinguishing feature is that it is a serial publication. This means that considerable efforts are put towards guaranteeing that individual titles are recognised over time, establishing continuity in the reader's mind. The character of a magazine's appearance and editorial content is, therefore, central to this. A central paradox of the magazine, however, is that as an industrial product remaining essentially the same from week to week or month to month, it must depend on novelty and change to encourage loyalty among readers, or attract new ones, if it is to prove a success.

The study of magazines might sound like a contradiction in terms. Unlike books, they are designed to be ephemeral. They are not repositories of knowledge intended to be pored over, reflected on and kept as treasures. Like newspapers, their outsize pages testify to an altogether more interrupted form of reading, they are not made to be treated with seriousness, and their political content is often covert. The quiet context of study is far removed from their original circulation, as part of the daily commute, in family life, or in dialogue with others. They bring to mind the pursuits of leisure, rather than work. Magazines also deviate from other printed sources in both content and appearance because editorials and advertisements, pictures and words are constantly competing for our attention.

Most commercially sold magazines result from a division of labour between editors, advertisers, journalists, illustrators, typographers, designers, art directors and, in more recent years, stylists. As such, magazine publishing is a complex area of study and the methods needed for its understanding cross a range of academic disciplines. Moreover, since magazines are composite rather than singular objects their character reflects different sources and disciplines. In this sense, they could be seen to parallel interiors, another form of complex designed entity, and in many respects they raise equivalent questions of interpretation. Indeed, the etymology of the word *magasin* from the French, reveals that both shop and publication lie in the same root of origin. The literature on the department store, another site of nineteenth-century consumption dependent on accumulation, diversity and distraction, is useful for establishing some of the key questions to be asked of magazines.[1]

The essays in this volume take a dual focus as their central theme: that of the design of magazines and the mediation of the idea of design through magazines. While the first appears straightforward, for the latter we must acknowledge that the period in question, the late nineteenth and twentieth centuries, was one of increasing self-consciousness about design and magazines were no exception in this. The aim underlying the selection of essays is to introduce a range of design history research methodologies while also offering new empirical material for the study of magazines. Perhaps because of their ambivalent status as ephemeral and potentially marginal forms, both as literature and as object, magazines have received relatively brief attention from historians concerned to identify their contribution to the design landscape. Nevertheless, design history, we suggest, is well-suited to do this, given its interest in

combining immanent analysis of objects with considerations of manufacture and consumption. Indeed, the cultural and economic concerns
that magazines hold in tension, their synthesis of image and text, even
their three-dimensionality, are ideal territory for the interdisciplinary
methods of design history.

The research undertaken by the contributors to this volume raises
interesting questions about the sources available for those concerned
to reconstruct the circumstances of design for magazine publication, its
material and methods, markets and consumers. As well as employing
the design historian's accepted tools of analysis, the research presented
here draws upon methodologies from fields as distinct as anthropology
and art history in order to identify how magazines construct ideologies
relating to concepts like gender, race and national identity. As research
material, magazines are also appealing, lest we forget, because they are
about the experience of consumption, which was – and is – mainly pleas-
urable, at least for those with some disposable income. Buying products
and using them contributes to our sense of identity; often reading about
products and about using them can also be fun.[2]

The essays have been selected from the work of the students and staff
on the V&A/RCA programme in the History of Design. In reviewing the
archive of work undertaken in recent years, it came to light that magazines were an increasingly important focus for a variety of approaches,
and that sufficient work now exists to warrant a volume dedicated to
them. Together, the essays offer a consideration of the landmarks in
modern magazine publishing through a series of case studies. The range
is far from definitive but instead suggests methods and approaches which
should be read as symptomatic of the concerns of the design historian
interested in understanding magazines and their impact on everyday life.
The particular focus of the essays reflects the strength of sources in the
form of library and archival material available for study and research in
London and beyond. It is also prompted by an agenda set by issues and
debates in design history, ones to do with Modernism and modernity,
consumer society, and culture and technology, which provide the broader
historical and theoretical frame for work included here.

The bias towards the Western design tradition, and in particular
Britain and the United States, it should be added, underlines where the
great power and resources lie, not only in terms of the initial production

of magazines, but also in their safekeeping for future generations. We would be among the first to acknowledge, however, that the next important and rewarding challenge will be to open these methods and questions to a more international range of study.

The essays are organised in three related sections: The magazine as designed object, Magazines and the consumer, and Promoting design through magazines. Together they consider the life-time of the modern magazine since around 1880. They trace the emergence of the modern, mass-market magazine as well as the specialist design periodicals, offering a range of perspectives which make a composite picture of the elements informing the shape and character of the modern magazine.

Early magazines and methodology

In order to situate the periodical in context, however, it is relevant to consider its earlier beginnings and to take a cursory glance at the history of printing. From the second half of the eighteenth century, factors such as the increase in population, expansion of trade, improved means of communication and advances in technology stimulated both the printing industry and the market. Print and typographic historian Michael Twyman deliberately omits books from his otherwise comprehensive history of printing, favouring instead the playing cards, devotional prints, reward notices, livestock sale posters, sheet music, tickets and other printed matter that flourished during the period.[3] It may be useful to see the magazine emerging from the ephemera he depicts, as much as from its more obvious precursors, the book and the newspaper. Twyman's study is also relevant for its consideration of the printing industry's historical structure, and the unsung labour force behind it. He charts for instance, the individual printer's progression through the nineteenth century from the generalist who might print everything from a visiting card to a local newspaper, to the highly specialised printers who would work only on packaging, or stationery, books and indeed magazines.

This same shift from the general to the specific may be observed in the way magazines themselves developed over time. At the beginning of the nineteenth century they were fairly general productions which sought to capture as wide a market as possible by including a mixture of comment on politics, social life, fashion, etiquette, religion and morality. The earliest specialist magazines were those aimed at women. First produced during the late 1800s, they identified a readership which remains crucial today. New titles were funded by advertising for goods that simultaneously became branded commodities. These very often depended on their graphic identity in press advertisements, just as much as in point of sale and poster designs in the wider world, contributing to what historian Thomas Richards has called 'the commodity culture' of late nineteenth-century society.[4] The process of diversification of target readers has continued since then, causing the commentators Tebbel and Zuckerman to note that there is now 'no interest known to mankind which does not have at least one magazine to serve it'.[5]

Given the sheer volume of material, only a few historians have attempted to provide comprehensive surveys of the magazine industries in England and America.[6] David Reed's history of the popular magazine in Britain and America limits its terms by laying emphasis on the magazine as a manufactured product, using this as a corrective to what he regards as overly literary or personalised histories. This is the magazine as a phenomenon born of technology and commerce. Reed, therefore, describes the conditions under which such a commodity might flourish, identifying increasing urbanisation as one of the key factors. Comparing Britain's continuing industrial development in the nineteenth century (which was linked to its coal industry of the eighteenth), to America's later explosion of industrial activity, he explains how both countries' populations came to be concentrated in cities. This shift resulted in significantly lowering the unit costs of distribution for all goods, including magazines. In turn, transportation systems both within and outside the urban centres developed to make them realistic working propositions. Railway systems resulted in faster postal services, which facilitated both business communication and the dissemination of magazines. The effect of these shifts in turn stimulated a remarkable growth in education, ensured the rise of public libraries; and instilled the habit of reading in an evolving middle class.

Inevitably, such surveys deal in generalisations rather than subtleties. Nonetheless, they acknowledge the economic concerns that drive the magazine publishing industry and the precise circumstances of its manufacture – the presses, paper production, typesetting machines, colour science and advances in mechanical illustration techniques, all of which had an important impact on the speed and facility with which magazines might be produced. One such landmark technology was the first web-fed rotary perfecting press installed at *The New York Sun* in 1865.[7] The machine brought about a great acceleration in production times because rolls of paper, the web, meant faster machines which printed on both sides simultaneously. Such an example reminds us of the materiality of magazines, as does Reed's description of the race to find a suitable vegetable source for paper which until the mid-nineteenth century was extracted from cotton and rag waste. After all, it is ultimately the differing qualities of paper that are the parameters defining many aspects of a modern publication's nature. The size, strength, flexibility and porosity of the paper are all things which affect the printing process and in turn, the reader's own experience of turning the pages.

Another significant development in magazine production was the introduction of the half-tone process as an illustrative technique. For most of the nineteenth century, wood engraving had been the basis of magazine illustrations, but it was an extremely costly and labour-intensive process. Half-tones, which use small specks of ink to create a delicate shading effect, were a radically cheaper alternative, taking hours rather than days to prepare. As an example, the high cost of engravings meant that the *Illustrated London News* cost sixpence in 1848, about half the day rate of a labourer, whereas fifty years later, the use of multiple illustrations was commonplace and the price had dropped to threepence.[8] As the century drew to a close, half-tone illustrations and, subsequently, the introduction of photography would change the appearance of magazines forever, heralding a new era dominated by the power of the image.

Magazines have often been viewed as unique historical resources for the historian because they record the incredibly complicated flow of life in a breadth of detail that is unavailable in any other medium. Tebbel and Zuckerman, for instance, point out that most of the visual images we have of America in the nineteenth century come from magazine pages that first displayed woodcuts and, in time, photography to illuminate the world. Their account of the American periodical is decidedly partisan, claiming it as possibly the 'most democratic institution the country has yet produced'.[9] The reason for their tribute is that whilst they emphasise the pivotal role that the magazine has played in promoting conformity and shaping consumer culture, they also see it as expressing the limitless interests of the most diverse population in the world. In order to demonstrate this, their wide-ranging volume covers several specialist as well as popular titles, including extensive discussions of the abolitionist press, African-American periodicals, children's magazines and story-papers. They, too, cite the emergence of the half-tone as a crucial technological factor in the magazine's history, linking it to the success of the 'muckrakers' – the magazines which flourished between 1895 and 1918 by running exposés of corruption within large corporations and government institutions. Not only were these publications sensational in content, they looked exciting and were rich with colour. Costing only a dime, instead of the usual 35 cents, they were part of a wave of magazines that was reaching a new American public with less education and less money than before.

As magazines diversified, the roles of those producing them also became more specialised. William Owen traces this division of labour in his study *Magazine Design*, citing Aubrey Beardsley as the first to be credited with the title 'art director' in the *Yellow Book* of 1894.[10] His is one of several accounts which identifies the magazine as a vehicle for the work of graphic designers, and asserts that design is a communicative rather than a decorative act.[11] Owen argues that because the early magazine lacked a unique visual format it became an ideal medium for graphic exploration. Focusing on the course of magazine design during the twentieth century, he identifies design protagonists from the fields of photojournalism, the Modern Movement in Europe and the underground press who all had an impact on the medium. Crucially he draws attention to the difference in American and European magazine design of the 1940s. Reeling from the effects of the Second World War, Europe's publishing business lacked not only resources but the market and advertisers to pay for it. Whilst editorial design was advancing steadily in the United States, in Europe, pulp weeklies were churning out escapist fiction and magazine producers were preoccupied by the need to conserve paper. Not until the post-war boom of the 1950s did the influence of American abstract expressionism, with its generosity of colour and space, really take hold in Europe.

Studies that focus on the aesthetics of magazines often function partly as reference manuals for those working in the field and partly as manifestos for the profession. Highlighting the role of the magazine designer, they uncover what is sometimes understood as a personal struggle to relinquish traditional book and newspaper typography and to create an entirely new medium of text and pictures. As a professional designer himself, Ruari McLean's studies in typographic history, for instance, stem from a desire to elevate the reputation of the business from craft to art.[12] Whilst this approach can usefully reconstruct the creative effort involved in the production of magazines, it risks overestimating the autonomy of the designer and misreading the endeavour as a chiefly aesthetic instead of commercial enterprise.

The same charge might be levelled at histories which have focused on editors and publishing magnates.[13] Whilst the particular skills and predilections of such characters certainly affected the magazines produced under their leadership, an overemphasis on individual personalities can obscure the fact that they are working within the constraints of cultural inheritances, economic relationships and technical boundaries. Salme Harju Steinberg's study of Edward Bok (editor of the hugely successful American periodical, *The Ladies' Home Journal*) is unusual in this context. Steinberg uses Bok to explore a wider theme, namely the uneasy coexistence of reform journalism with an increasingly powerful advertising presence in the late nineteenth and early twentieth-century magazine. Steinberg never loses sight of the magazine as a double proposition, registering that its success was due to its ability to conform to the needs of both advertisers and readers. Her work identifies a relationship of compromise which is at the heart of most modern magazines.

The significance of advertising to magazines is indicated by the fact that before the advent of radio in 1920s America, the periodical press was the only way to reach a national audience. (In England newspapers as well as magazines carried advertising.) From the early nineteenth century, industrialists realised they could translate the new pursuit of reading into consuming, by building direct relationships with the market through increasingly sophisticated printed salesmanship. The interdependence of the publishing and promotional industries has ensured that many of the most insightful commentaries on modern magazine history are to be found in studies of advertising.[14] The conversion of readers to consumers has also been the subject of several recent studies, many of which focus on the magazine's cultivation of a mass female market.[15] It is a salutary thought that the only reliable figures we have concerning magazine circulation come from institutions such as the Association of American

Advertisers, formed in 1899 to drag out accurate statistics from periodical publishers. In this sense, even the most objective aspects of magazine history are always and inextricably linked to the commercial sphere.

Other methodologies

Moving to those studies which are predominantly concerned with the contents of magazines, they usually divide between those which analyse the text and those which give priority to images, whether in advertisements or editorial pages.[16] A number of sociologically informed interpretations have focused on how particular groups of people and sectors of society make use of magazines or how they can shape aspirations. Through such an approach, reading magazines becomes an active form of cultural production. The first inroads towards understanding magazines and valuing them as a form of literature in Britain was signalled in Richard Hoggart's seminal book, *The Uses of Literacy*, a study of working-class life, first published in 1957.[17] This tradition was continued in cultural studies by Raymond Williams, whose impressive study, *The Long Revolution* (1961) was also formative for the analysis it gave of the mechanisms of popular publishing, part of what Williams saw as a continuation of the project of the Enlightenment.[18] Williams's approach, it should be added, concentrated on the textual. An equal consideration of the visual and textual was introduced in the work of Dick Hebdige and Angela McRobbie, whose respective studies of magazines directly marketed towards youth sub-cultures and teenage girls applied a cultural studies approach to more contemporary material.[19] In this and much subsequent work, a fluent reading of the allure of magazines was key. Unlike design history, however, cultural studies rarely engages with the circumstances of production, the design process or the material qualities of the magazines.

Many of the essays in this volume, by dealing with magazines, develop an understanding of gender and design. An enduring legacy of the Frankfurt School on interpretations of popular culture has been to disparage areas of consumption associated with the female sphere.[20] And too often in this tradition, women have been cast as passive consumers, duped by the forces of persuasion into pursuing false needs and desires. The extent to which a magazine can function as a reliable source of information rather than distraction therefore becomes a contested issue. In general, the literature on magazines varies as to whether it sees magazines as a source of manipulation of desire or fount of useful knowledge, or indeed both. Either way, it is a question that none can avoid.

With this in mind, it is possibly not surprising that women's magazines were all too often treated with a lack of seriousness in academic circles. It was not until 1970 that Cynthia White, a sociologist, published the first complete study of women's magazines, which laid down important foundations for much subsequent work.[21] The emphasis of this work was to plot the circulation histories of leading American and British magazines against broad social and cultural changes in women's lives. A central issue addressed in this study is whether magazines could be said to reflect the experience of women beyond their pages.

Through the bringing together of women's studies and literature studies, magazines have been recognised as a central element in women's lives, in work that has explored their intrinsic ambivalence. This has predominantly been through studies of individual titles, such as Jennifer Scanlon's account of the leading American women's title, *The Ladies' Home Journal*, and the thematic interpretation of how magazines engaged with issues of gender, home and leisure.[22] Interestingly, much of the pioneering work in this field has concentrated on the late nineteenth and early twentieth centuries in Britain and America – a time when many of these structures first came in to being on such a scale. These studies are concerned wherever possible to reconstruct the reader. In a work such as Ellen Gruber Garvey's, *The Adman in the Parlor: Magazines and the Gendering of Consumer Culture, 1880s to 1910s*, the approach taken is a close literary reading of the editorial pages, letter pages and the mode of address made to the reader, in the form of the advertisements.[23] Her study reveals that 'reading' was far from a passive activity. Rather, young women readers used magazines to inform their hobbies; collecting or cutting and pasting them, and incorporating their newly gained knowledge in their domestic lives in ways that magazine proprietors could not have predicted.

In turn, women's involvement as professionals in the magazine industry has also received interpretation, especially in the case of the United States. Ellen Mazur Thomson has traced the engagement of women art directors and designers in American graphic design from 1870 to 1920.[24] Michelle Bogart studied the place of women as illustrators for mainstream periodicals and the hierarchies and terms of employment in the early twentieth century.[25] And in at least one case, the life and work of a pioneering woman art director, Cipe Pineles, who was active in mid-century America as a designer of women and teenage girl magazines, has now been researched.[26]

A central concern in the literature on magazines, therefore, is their relationship with their consumers, the readers. Were readers simply recipients of what the editors or magazine proprietors fed them, or could the relationship be more complex, one of negotiation and possible dissent? While magazines were an imaginative space full of potential, did they in fact reinforce traditional stereotypes, and present deeply conservative attitudes? In Chapter 5, Trevor Keeble examines such a tension through a case study of how modernist design was represented by the popular consumer magazine *Woman* in 1950s Britain. He suggests that the magazine formed a vehicle for a less doctrinaire approach to home decoration and design than that taken in official publications, such as *Design* magazine and its architectural counterparts. In such a context, Keeble asks whether an appeal to popular taste should be seen as a design compromise.

Most magazines depend on revenue from advertising to pay their staff and to produce the publication. Among the exceptions are subsidised ventures which can often afford to be more selective in their approach to advertising and employ alternative strategies in their editorial contents. Chapters 8 and 9 consider the magazines *Design* and *Crafts*. Both were British titles, published by their respective professional organisations and supported by government funding. Therefore, they did not require direct sales at the newsagent for their income but were rather monthly subscription journals aimed at specialist, professional readers. In many ways these two magazines acted as arbiters of taste and discrimination, guiding the reader, often in an institution or company rather than a private individual, in matters of commission or buying. The two contributions indicate how these unusual circumstances affected the nature of each journal.

Along with the approaches outlined above, if the interpretation of magazines is to go beyond generic classification and deal with specific instances, a form of immanent analysis of imagery is needed. Traditional art history does not provide a model of approach here, so instead, in recent years, design history has turned to visual culture studies.[27] With translations of French theoretical writings on culture becoming available, the interpretation of magazines experienced what has been called a 'linguistic turn' in the 1970 and 1980s. In particular, Roland Barthes' writing was especially influential on a generation who were developing approaches to popular culture. Barthes' theoretical essay 'Myth Today' and shorter analyses of examples of cultural representations assembled in the book *Mythologies* first became available in English translation in 1973.[28] One of Barthes' most poignant examples was a photographic image of an Algerian soldier saluting the French flag, the *tricoleur* at the time of the Algerian coup, from the cover of the popular weekly magazine, *Paris Match*. He revealed how popular imagery can work ideologically to incorporate accepted social values and political beliefs, making them appear natural. While so doing, he developed a set of influential theoretical concepts and specialist terminology. Barthes and other French thinkers led more generally to a tradition of deconstruction and decoding of photographic imagery in advertising and magazines.[29] The advantage of the semiological method is that it offers ways to interpret encoded meanings in magazines and understand desire and pleasure of the text. It has been applied most successfully to systems of representation that deal with fashion, style and sexuality. The potential danger for the historian is that it can present the object of study, in this case the magazine, in a form of the continuous present while overlooking the specific circumstances of manufacture and intention.

As Zoe Whitley's essay (Chapter 6) on fashion photography of black models in British *Vogue* indicates, design history is concerned to combine theoretical interpretation with information about the specific instances of representation gained from empirical research. Among the empirical methods available to the design historian is what is known as content analysis, a model drawn from the social sciences and employed in media studies.[30] This can be useful if the historian of the magazine wishes to establish a representative point of view. It allows for moving beyond the interpretation of a particular issue of a magazine to establish a narrative that does justice to its changes over time. In this connection, it is useful to distinguish between a diachronic study, which seeks to explain change over time and the synchronic, which focuses on a single moment or a cross-section.[31] Most historians accept that adopting a quantitative approach can be helpful when dealing with change over time. In the case of magazines, research can start by taking a broad survey of a title and then a decision is made to pursue sampling based on regular intervals over a number of years, applying the same criteria of analysis. This method is used by Marie-Louise Bowallius, for example, in her study of the changes in colour printing in the popular American magazine *The Woman's Home Companion* (Chapter 1). Through this approach, Bowallius is able to show that it was through advertising, rather than editorial initiatives that colour illustrations in magazines were introduced in the 1920s.

While the role of magazines in fuelling the economy is clear, their history has also witnessed attempts to subvert the status quo. One familiar strategy was the use of graphic satire and caricature, which goes back, at least, to eighteenth-century Britain.[32] In Chapter 3, Emily King explores the overtly political London-based listings magazine, *Time Out*. Here, design was used as a crucial marker of distinction, introducing the publication as an alternative to mainstream publishing, defining its cultural space through the choice of cover design and approach to layout more generally.

Design historians are attentive to the changes in design layout as one of the most significant elements of a magazine. For instance, change or continuity of a title's masthead, as discussed by Garland and Naylor in relation to *Design* magazine, suggests how attitudes to the title as a whole can be conveyed. Similarly, a change of typeface or the introduction of a grid to reorganise the page layout of a magazine may be important in design history but overlooked by other kinds of interpretation. The appointment of a new editor or art director, as Linda Sandino shows, can herald an entirely new identity for a magazine. And in another essay (Chapter 2), Jeremy Aynsley explores the sensitivity shown towards type in the inter-war period in Europe, when interesting crossovers occurred between the specialist type and graphics press and high profile fashion magazines, helping to define a commercial graphic idiom.

Another established method within design history is to use the interview as a source of oral testimony. In Britain, many of the principal methods of gathering oral evidence for historical purposes have been outlined in Paul Thompson's work, which emphasises social history.[33] In order to establish a history of magazines, for example, interviews with key figures are sometimes the only way in which the everyday workings of a magazine can be retrieved. Several of the essays in this volume depend on such evidence, for instance, King, Sandino and Whitley all interviewed important members of staff from the magazines of their chosen study. By contrast, the conversation between Gillian Naylor, journalist turned design historian, and Ken Garland, designer, each an example of what has been called the 'reflective practitioner', offers the opportunity to locate specific details about the circumstances of the thinking behind *Design* magazine.[34] The conversation (Chapter 8), reveals how complex, yet also how rewarding, the process to reconstruct the history and significance of magazines can be. Along with the other essays in this volume, it bears testimony to the rich cultural questions presented by the design and publication of the modern magazine.

Notes

1 See M. B. Miller, *The Bon Marché: Bourgeois Culture and the Department Store, 1869–1920* (London: Allen & Unwin, 1981); R. Williams, *Dream Worlds: Mass-consumption in Late Nineteenth Century France* (Berkeley, Oxford: University of California Press, 1982), and E. D. Rappaport, *Shopping for Pleasure: Women in the Making of London's West End* (Princeton, NJ and Chichester: Princeton University Press, 2000).

2 This idea is explored by H. Damon-Moore, in *Magazines for the Millions: Gender and Commerce in the Ladies' Home Journal and the Saturday Evening Post, 1880–1910* (Albany: State University of New York Press, 1994).

3 M. Twyman, *Printing: 1770–1970: An Illustrated History of its Development and uses in England* (London: Eyre & Spottiswoode, 1970).

4 T. Richards, *The Commodity Culture of Victorian Britain: Advertising and Spectacle, 1851–1914* (London: Verso, 1991).

5 J. Tebbel and M. E. Zuckerman, *The Magazine in America, 1741–1990* (New York and Oxford: Oxford University Press, 1991), p. 244.

6 See D. Reed, *The Popular Magazine in Britain and the United States, 1880–1960* (British Library: London, 1997), and Tebbel and Zuckerman, *The Magazine in America*.

7 Reed, *The Popular Magazine*, p. 43.

8 Cited by William Owen, *Magazine Design* (London: Laurence King, 1991).

9 Tebbel and Zuckerman, *The Magazine in America*, p. 382.

10 Owen, *Magazine Design*, p. 13.

11 See also, R. McLean, *Magazine Design* (London: Oxford University Press, 1969); P. Jobling and D. Crowley, *Graphic Design: Reproduction and Representation since 1800* (Manchester and New York: Manchester University Press, 1996); D. Crowley, *Magazine Covers* (London: Mitchell Beazley, 2003).

12 Ruari McLean, *Typography* (London: Thames & Hudson, 1980); and *How Typography Happens* (London: The British Library and Oak Knoll Press, 2000).

13 See, for instance, C. Seebohm, *The man who was Vogue: The Life and Times of Condé Nast* (London: Weidenfeld & Nicolson, 1982) and Salme Harju Steinberg, *Reformer in the Marketplace: Edward W. Bok and The Ladies' Home Journal* (Baton Rouge and London: Louisiana State University Press, 1979).

14 See, for instance, S. Strasser, *Satisfaction Guaranteed: The Making of the Mass Market* (New York: Pantheon Books, 1989), and R. Marchand, *Advertising the American Dream: Making Way for Modernity 1920–1940* (Berkeley: University of California Press, 1986).

15 M. Beetham, *A Magazine of Her Own? Domesticity and Desire in the Woman's Magazine 1800–1914* (London: Routledge, 1996); J. Scanlon, *Inarticulate Longings: The Ladies' Home Journal, Gender, and the Promises of Consumer Culture* (New York: Routledge, 1995), and Damon-Moore, *Magazines for the Millions*.

16 See M. Beetham, *A Magazine of Her Own?* and J. Winship, *Advertising in Women's Magazines, 1956–74* (Birmingham: Centre for Contemporary Cultural Studies, University of Birmingham, 1980).

17 R. Hoggart, *The Uses of Literacy* (Harmondsworth: Penguin, 1958).

18 R. Williams, *The Long Revolution* (Harmondsworth: Penguin, 1965).

19 D. Hebdige, *Hiding in the Light: On Images and Things* (London: Comedia, 1988); A. McRobbie, *Feminism and Youth Culture: From Jackie to Just Seventeen* (Basingstoke: Macmillan, 1991).

20 W. Schirmacher (ed.), *German 20th Century Philosophy: The Frankfurt School* (New York: Continuum, 2000).

21 C. L. White, *Women's Magazines 1693–1968* (London: Michael Joseph, 1970).

22 J. Scanlon, *Inarticulate Longings* and Ros Ballaster et al., *Women's Worlds: Ideology, Femininity and the Woman's Magazine* (London: Macmillan, 1991).

23 E. G. Garvey, *The Adman in the Parlor: Magazines and the Gendering of Consumer Culture, 1880s to 1910s* (Oxford: Oxford University Press, 1996).

24 E. M. Thomson, *The Origins of Graphic Design History* (New Haven and London: Yale University Press, 1997).

25 M. H. Bogart, *Artists, Advertising and the Borders of Art* (Chicago: University of Chicago Press, 1995).

26 M. Scotford, *Cipe Pineles: A Life of Design* (New York and London: W. W. Norton, 1999).

27 J. Evans and S. Hall (eds), *Visual Culture: The Reader* (London: Sage in association with Open University, 1999).

28 R. Barthes, *Mythologies*, edited and translated by A. Lavers (London: Vintage, 1993), and *Image, Music, Text*, edited and translated by S. Heath (London: Fontana, 1977).

29 See, for example, J. Williamson, *Decoding Advertisements* (London: Marion Boyars, 1978); S. Nixon, *Hard Looks: Masculinities, Spectatorship and Contemporary Consumption* (London: UCL Press, 1996), and P. Jobling, *Fashion Spreads: Word and Image in Fashion Photography since 1980* (Oxford: Berg, 1999).

30 J. Fiske, *An Introduction to Communication Studies* (London: Methuen, 1982).

31 E. H. Carr, *What is History?* (Harmondsworth: Penguin, 1987). For the specific implications for design history, see J. A. Walker, *Design History and the History of Design* (London: Pluto Press, 1989), pp. 78–81.

32 See, for instance, D. Donald, *The Age of Caricature: The Age of Satirical Prints in the Reign of George III* (New Haven and London: published for the Paul Mellon Centre for Studies in British Art by Yale University Press, 1996).

33 P. Thompson, *Voice of the Past: Oral History* (Oxford: Oxford University Press, 1978).

34 D. A. Schön, *The Reflective Practitioner: How Professionals Think in Action* (Aldershot: Avebury, 1991).

Part I

The magazine as designed object

The immanent analysis of an object, taking into account the means by which it came into being, is a central concern of the design historian. In the case of magazines, this entails an understanding of the relationship between the design decisions and the technologies available to the magazine publisher, picture editor and designer. The three essays in this part concentrate on different elements within a magazine's composition, taken from different historical moments in the twentieth century. The first applies a quantitative approach to assess the balance between the use of colour illustrations to advertising and editorial pages. It focuses on the seminal period when colour was first introduced to magazines in the 1920s in the United States, as a forerunner to international change. The second essay casts a broad cultural view on the relation between typographic discourse and European Modernism in the inter-war years and suggests how this might be understood in attitudes towards magazine layout and design. The third essay develops an argument about the interpretation of design based on the testimony of the art director of a single magazine title, in this case, *Time Out* the London listings magazine of the 1970s, when design was used to signify an ideological position. Each essay testifies to the importance of paying close attention to the visual components of magazines: type, image and their interaction. What emerges is that design decisions about the appearance of a magazine layout can be informed by a number of aesthetic, economic, political and social forces.

1 ✧ Advertising and the use of colour in *Woman's Home Companion*, 1923–33

Marie-Louise Bowallius

T HIS ESSAY examines design changes in *Woman's Home Companion* magazine during the period 1923–33. The magazine was one of the biggest selling women's magazines in America in the early twentieth century with a circulation reaching over 1,200,000 in 1920. Aiming at the mass of American middle-class women, its strategies and appearance were distinct from those of the more upmarket magazines like *Vogue* and *Vanity Fair*. Consequently, its design has never attracted attention from design historians, who have tended to concentrated on stylistic developments and the Modern Movement's influence on magazine design.

By treating the magazine as a physical object, keeping in mind its role as a commodity as well as a cultural artefact, it is hoped that this analysis offers a way to understand how the design of a magazine creates meaning in a specific cultural context. Special attention is paid to how colour was used in the magazine during the period under review since 1920s America saw a huge upsurge in the use of colour-printing. While general design changes have been recorded by close observation of whole volumes of the magazine, the examination of its use of colour is based on studies of typical issues from the years 1923–33. The result is presented in quantitative as well as qualitative terms and interpreted against developments in culture, technology and economy, as well as the magazine's content and publishing history.

Publishing history: facts and figures

The *Woman's Home Companion* (hereafter called the *Companion*), began as a mail-order monthly, a publication whose primary function was to display cheap advertisements for even cheaper merchandise that could be secured by a small sum sent through the post.[1] Originally called *The Home*, the magazine led a precarious existence until it was taken over by the firm of Mast, Crowell & Kirkpatrick in 1883, a publishing company that had its roots in the manufacturing of agricultural machinery and already owned a magazine called *Farm and Fireside*. Soon after the acquisition, the general manager, John S. Crowell, decided that the women's page in *Farm and Fireside* was so popular that it suggested a much larger audience. *The Home* was converted into a women's magazine called the *Ladies' Home Companion*. Gradually its content was developed, and by 1890 the magazine had 100,000 subscribers.[2]

Its closest rival was the *Ladies' Home Journal* (hereafter called the *Journal*). Under the management of the publisher Cyrus H. K. Curtis it had developed from a column in a weekly agricultural newspaper to a big-selling women's magazine in the 1880s and became the clear leader in the race to develop mass-market female audiences in America in the late nineteenth century.[3] At a time when a big-selling magazine was one with a circulation of 100,000, the *Journal* sold 1 million in November 1889. But a decade later the *Companion* was openly competing with the *Journal* and slowly approached its sales numbers. Perhaps sensing that the similarity of his magazine's title to Curtis' was not helping, Crowell changed its name in 1897, replacing 'Ladies'' with 'Woman's'. The explicit motivation was that whereas 'woman' was an honest Anglo-Saxon word without a synonym, 'lady' retained slightly vulgar connotations.[4] It could be that Crowell perceived a class issue behind the change; 'lady' was more appealing to women from the upper class, whilst 'woman' was a word with which the middle-class readership identified more easily. 'Woman' or 'women' were also the terms used in the editorial pages.

In 1906 Crowell sold the company to three partners, of which Joseph Palmer Knapp was the majority shareholder. Under his management the *Companion* continued the competition for large circulations and by 1920 it was selling 1,215,069 a month.[5] Sales continued to increase and by 1931 the *Companion* took the circulation leadership of the women's monthlies from the *Journal*, by a matter of about 25,000 sales per month, at 2,606,123.[6]

Editorial staff and profile

During its career the *Companion* emerged as the closest to the *Journal* in its content and editorial viewpoint. In 1903 Gertrude Battles Lane was employed as household editor, a fact that caused some merriment in her house, where she was noted for her lack of interest in housekeeping. But she had some publishing experience, knew how to get the information she lacked, and was successful in creating loyalty among the readers. In 1911 she was appointed editor-in-chief, a post she held until her death in 1941. In the women's magazines' circulation wars of the 1930s she led the magazine to the first placing. Her success prompted Joseph Knapp to give her an ambiguous compliment, calling her 'the best man in the business'.[7]

What Lane did for the *Companion* was to focus the magazine firmly on women's topics, presenting articles from the woman's point of view. In a *Companion* promotion piece she presented her view of this woman and shared what her view on the readers meant for her editing work:

> In editing the *Woman's Home Companion*, I keep constantly in mind a picture of the housewife of today as I see her. She is not the woman who wants to do *more* housework, but the woman who wants to do *less* housework so that she will have more time for other things. She is intelligent and clearheaded. I must tell her the truth. She is busy; I must not waste her time. She is forever seeking new ideas: I must keep her in touch with the best. Her horizon is ever extending, her interests broadening, the pages of the *Woman's Home Companion* must reflect the sanest and most constructive thought on the vital issues of the day.[8]

By 1920, the *Companion* was quite capable of running articles on the forthcoming presidential campaign while also covering women in politics. The magazine followed a broad agenda, balancing the arts against social commentaries, fashion against needlework and cookery, with fiction as the dominating sector, taking just under 40 per cent of the magazine's editorial space in the first half of 1920.[9]

While celebrated authors were assigned to write stories, 'recognized authorities in what is now the science of home-making' were responsible for the *Companion*'s practical pages.[10] But Lane recognised that in order to succeed, a woman's magazine must acknowledge that women had many interests outside the home. In the November issue of 1933, for instance, the magazine talked about 'the emergence of women' through higher education, a broad movement in which the significance of the 'brilliant career' of the *Woman's Home Companion* was said to lie. In an article called 'Going Like Sixty' it took pride in having led, counselled and encouraged women towards achievement.

Throughout the years, the magazine made great efforts in establishing an air of intimacy between its readers and its editorial staff. It carried many pieces about what it called its own 'family' of authors, and printed reams of letters from readers, who wrote in to various columns and editors with questions, opinions and advice. As Christopher Wilson has pointed out, close contacts with the readers both enlarged and assured the continuity of readership and provided the germ for market research.[11] Letters gauged response and helped plan future content; replies reinforced the magazine's 'intimacy' and advisory role – institutional strategies that also served the business interests of the publisher in an efficient way. The seemingly personal voice – colloquial, forceful and direct – thus had more than one function. In the shift toward mass-consumer capitalism it was also one of the means by which middle-class women were persuaded to surrender to the pleasures of consumption.

Cultural background and ideology

> In no other country in the world are there such magazines as the *Woman's Home Companion*. There could not be, because the factors to call them into being exist only here.[12]

Historian William Leach has described a shift in the American culture from around 1880 toward a secular business and market-oriented culture, with the exchange and circulation of money and goods as the foundation of aesthetic life and moral sensibility.[13] Until 1930, Leach argues, this movement allowed for only one vision of the good life and gradually dispensed with all others. Its cardinal features were: acquisition and consumption as the means of achieving happiness; the cult of the new; the democratisation of desire; and money value as the predominant measure of all value in society. At the centre of the cult of the new were fashion and style.

There can be little doubt that magazines like the *Companion* and the *Journal* had a role to play in bringing these cultural shifts about. Through their financial dependence on advertising and editorial commitment to consumerist capitalism, they were constantly reflecting what has been regarded as the heart of American culture in the modern period. Ideologically they have been given a place in publishing history as conservative spokesmen for the role of women in society and patriotic defenders of American values and the republic's involvement in the First World War.[14] In the early 1930s they educated their readers to be patriotic consumers of manufactured goods. In 1932, the *Journal* promoted an 'enlightened self-interest' through 'pocket-book patriotism' as a means to end the economic Depression that had started with the Wall Street crash in October 1929.[15] In a special article called 'It's up to the women', the *Journal* presented seven points for prosperity – a programme of spending, which constituted the platform of American Economists Committee for Women's Activities. It was supported by Mrs Franklin D. Roosevelt herself and the presidents of organisations like the National Federation of Business and Professional Women's Clubs, the National League of Women Voters, National Council of Jewish Women, and the International Federation of Catholic Alumnae.[16] Arguing that greater consumption on everyone's part meant lower prices for individuals, the magazine also promoted the democratisation of desire, which according to the editors meant greater freedom for everyone. Just like its closest rival, the *Companion* ran editorials touting the virtues of advertising, guaranteed that their advertisers were trustworthy and reliable and never tried to hide the fact that the growth of national advertising was a crucial factor for its successful career:

Advertising

It is a tribute to the shrewdness of the founders of the *Companion* that they saw so immediately the approach of the great wave of national advertising which was to inform women widely and swiftly of their growing freedom and was also to make possible a new type of magazine, generous in content and low in price. For it was the rise of national advertising that brought the modern magazine to birth and has fostered its amazing expansion.[17]

Under the management of Joseph Knapp and his editor-in-chief, Gertrude Lane, the *Companion* attracted $6 million in advertising revenue and 1,215,069 readers in 1920. In 1931 the advertising revenue had risen to $10,187,101 and the monthly circulation had increased to 2,606,123. The magazine's cover price was 10 cents, from which follows that about 76 per cent of the income came from selling advertising space in 1920 while 24 per cent came from newsstand sales and subscriptions. In 1931 the advertising revenue made up to 70 per cent of the total income, which reflected a general trend towards a greater financial reliance on sales figures. But what made the ability to attract readers of crucial financial importance was the fact that advertisers inevitably flocked to magazines with large circulations.

Among the major advertisers were manufacturers of food, cleansers and washing powders, cosmetics and hygiene articles, and articles for the home-maker, such as towels, blankets, kitchenware, carpets and lino-leum floors. These were the manufacturers producing relatively cheap consumer goods that were within the reach of the *Companion's* female middle-class readers. The most expensive advertising spaces were bought to advertise products like Old Dutch and Bon Ami cleansing powders, Wheatena whole wheat, Woodbury's Facial Soap, Dillbury Pancake Flour, and 3-minute Oat Flakes, and in the early 1930s ads for General Electric Refrigerators appeared on the inside of the back covers. Food manufacturers dominated the magazine's full-page ads with full colour illustrations of branded products like Campbell's Soups, Jell-O, Wesson Oil, Crisco, Del Monte, Dole, Kellogg's and Swift's. Among the faithful full-page advertisers we also find Listerine, Pond's, and Colgate with advertisements for a huge array of hygiene and beauty articles.

Altogether, 47–56 per cent of the magazine's space was used for advertising in the period under review.[18] Hence, 44–53 per cent consisted of the *Companion's* typical mix of fiction, fashion and domestic matters, interspersed with special articles on burning issues, such as the responsibilities of the female consumers during the depression.

Editorial material

While the advertisements represented the ever-expanding empire of new consumer goods, the content and tone of the editorial material can be described as a comfortable mixture of new and familiar material. To its readers, the *Companion* often represented an old and recognisable tradition, especially through the quantity of its fiction, offering the magazine as a means to achieve a sense of belonging in a rapidly changing world:

> In a world of gas logs and electricity somebody has to keep the home fires burning all year round. And those whose task this is find a helpful ally in the *Woman's Home Companion* – the gift that comes again and again, with new usefulness and delight ... When you give the *Companion*, you are giving ... wonderful serials and scores of exciting short stories, to read in the long winter evenings and the warm summer afternoons ... And when you send the *Companion* you can say: 'Let's read this year, together. Let's look together at the same lovely covers, and turn the pages at the same time. We'll laugh at the same funny things, and enjoy the same stories, and wonder together what's going to happen to the heroine next month ... you and I will be thinking of the same things, so we'll *think together.*'[19]

Thus proposing to fill the gap that had occurred when old-fashioned forms of communities had disappeared, the magazine offered a way to enter new forms of communions. From a society based on religious beliefs, America was developing a secular 'culture of desire', in which the consumption of goods and sentimental stories were offered as means to achieve 'salvation'.[20] In the formation of this new culture, the *Companion* had a role to play. To a great extent it was fulfilled through its financial and editorial strategies and its content, but a close examination of its design reveals that the look of the magazine also played its part.

Design and production technology

In the publishing industry of today covers are regarded as a form of package, competing with others in the marketplace and promoting magazines through headlines of editorial content and visual appeal.

This has not always been the case. Magazine covers were first specially designed for each issue in the 1890s and their early format was heavily influenced by poster design. As awareness of the cover's selling power grew, some magazines adopted methods used in advertising, but the appeal was above all credited to the quality of the illustrations. Great efforts were made to engage the most recognised artists and illustrators, and journals like the *Ladies' Home Journal* and *Saturday Evening Post* were important in shaping the contours of illustrators' identities and of commercial art practice at the turn of the century in America. According to Michele Bogart, they helped to establish illustration as both 'a prestigious high-profile form of art' and an attractive career option.[21] In 1901 the *Journal* offered reprints of their cover illustrations (without text) for sale to the public, arguing that if framed they were 'works of art fit to hang beside any painting'.[22] Bogart suggests that these kinds of practices contributed to a blurring of borders between art and illustration on the part of the general public, who framed the pictures and for whom such covers signified 'art'. At the same time, cover illustrations functioned as advertisements for the magazines themselves. As such, they represented a crucial shift 'from an older ideal of illustration as purely artistic medium to its newer purpose as instrument and expression of consumerist commercial values'.[23]

While upmarket magazines like American *Vogue* demonstrated a clear commitment to European art in the 1920s, the covers of the *Companion* carried realistic illustrations by American artists. In spite of a gradual simplification, their style had to do with a national tradition more than with European concepts of art, which seems appropriate in regards to the magazine's patriotism. Often they presented images of the ideal American woman and her family. Sometimes she was devoting her time to leisure activities outside the home, but most of the time she happily carried out her duties to the family, engaged in 'the science of home-making'. Traditional American values of womanhood and family life were constantly reflected and, to a lesser extent, so too was the relative freedom women had acquired for activities outside the home.

The *Companion* kept the same format, 260 × 340 mm, throughout the period concerned. The number of pages varied, presumably according to the advertising department's ability to attract advertisers for each issue. Variations spanned from 110 to 180 pages. The average issue consisted of 150 pages, while the *Journal* sometimes produced as many as 260 pages.

The front-of-the-book section was dominated by fiction, special articles and columns interspersed with full-page ads. Small advertisements were confined to the back pages. Short stories and other editorial features were cut up and ran into columns further back in the magazine, thus helping to draw the reader's attention to those ads which otherwise were easy to ignore – a strategy also used by the *Journal* to please the advertisers.

While fiction and fashion were almost exclusively illustrated with drawings, photographs were used for special articles on gardening, cooking, house decoration and women's role in society. This probably resulted from the tendency to attribute to photographs a literal matter-of-fact realism, while the more sentimental drawings were considered to be appropriate fiction and fashion illustrations. The *Companion* engaged several of the famous illustrators used by prestigious magazines like *Vogue*. Eduardo Benito and Georges Lepape both contributed fashion drawings to the magazine, but story illustrations were entrusted to American illustrators within a tradition of realism – sometimes witty, but predominantly sentimental. Among the names mentioned were R.M.Crosby, Pruett Carter, Carolyn Edmondson, Martha Sawyers and Norman Rockwell – the most famous of them all (see Figure 1.1).

Throughout the period, gradual improvements were made to the typography and layout. Compared to the *Journal*, the *Companion* was more successful in modernising its appearance. The columns of text were gradually being given more space and the typography was simplified. Despite a similar striving towards a more minimal graphic style, the *Journal* still looked rather old-fashioned in 1930. With an elaborate script for its headings, its typography contrasted with the *Companion*'s, where a much simpler, serif style was used at that time. Even so, the *Companion* was less radical in applying modernist design principles compared to several other magazines. It did not make use of white space or sans serif typefaces like *Vogue*, and its devotion to photography was never comparable to *Vanity Fair*. Asymmetry was used cautiously in the layout and photographs and illustrations were treated in a conservative fashion.

With few exceptions, photographs in the early 1920s were submitted to what has been called 'art treatment', in other words, they were

1.1 Short story illustrated by Norman Rockwell, *Woman's Home Companion*, November 1933.

surrounded by frames which clearly defined them from the rest of the page. The photographs were made to resemble artworks or family portraits. In this way a new (and cheaper) illustration technique was helped to acceptance through familiar modes of presentation.

In the early 1930s the *Companion*'s Art Director, Henry Quinan, preferred his artwork and even photographs to bleed out into the white space of the unadorned page surface.[24] This allowed the eye to move much more freely across the surface and sustained an illusion that the page was larger. But unlike Mehemed Fehmy Agha at *Vogue*, he never allowed his pictures to bleed out to the edge of the page before 1933. As this technique is often said to be a characteristic feature of modern magazine design Quinan's strategy can once again be described as a middle way between modern and old-fashioned.[25] In this environment of a gradually modernised magazine, where 'new' techniques were balanced with 'familiar' ones, colour was increasingly used in the *Companion* during the 1920s and early 1930s.

The use of colour

The exploitation of colour was an important ingredient in a new commercial aesthetic which took shape in America from the 1880s onwards. During this period merchants took command over colour, glass and light, fashioning a strong link between them and consumption. The exploitation of colour took many forms. Advertising historian, Roland Marchand describes 'the colour explosion' in advertising and consumer goods in the 1920s.[26] During this decade colour was introduced in a long array of products, such as telephones, pencils, towels, cars, and kitchen and bathroom accessories. But, according to Marchand, the manufacturers of consumer goods had to be convinced that their products belonged to the realm of 'fashion' goods before they were willing to introduce a choice of colours in their products. In this process the advertising agents played a key role. In their search for something 'new' about the products advertised, they discovered colour as one obvious method of creating a sense of style and novelty. They also recognised the value colour had in attracting attention to the advertising page. The result of this was that whilst an issue in 1923 included colour on every fourth page, an issue in 1933 had colour on every second page, although it should be noted that colour did not increase in an entirely regular way.

The earliest and most obvious use of colour in the *Companion* was the printing of full-colour covers (Figure 1.2). While ignoring European art tendencies and the 'zig-zag art' influenced by modern movements such as cubism, futurism, expressionism and surrealism, the magazine made sure that coloured cover illustrations created a sense of novelty and 'stylishness' on every issue. Given the selling power of the cover and the successful career of the magazine, the strategy seems to have been successful in attracting new subscribers amongst American middle-class women.

In relation to the sequential structure of the magazine, colour was first confined to the front-of-the-book section, where it was most immediately observed by the reader. As we have seen, this section was dominated by illustrated stories and full-page ads, while the back pages carried small ads and the continuations of articles and stories from the front section. In a typical issue of 1923 there was no colour whatsoever after page 120 in a 160-page magazine.[27]

The spread of four-colour prints throughout the magazine was partially determined by technical parameters. Since they were printed by photogravure and demanded a better quality paper, they were printed on separate presses on another paper stock than the rest of the magazine; hence they always occurred in pairs; on the front and back of the same page.

However, as paper and printing technology improved, the freedom to use colour more freely increased. In 1933 a better quality paper was introduced throughout the magazine, and a larger part of the pages was

1.2 *Woman's Home Companion,* June 1931.

printed photogravure. Four-colour illustrations started to appear on the same sheets as one-colour prints. At the same time colour invaded the back pages. Besides giving way for technological explanations, these changes can be interpreted as the result of a negotiation between editorial and advertising needs to create a sense of 'style' and draw attention to their material.

In 1923, 45 per cent of the full page ads in the *Companion* contained colour, increasing to about 67 per cent by 1929. As the major advertisers were food manufacturers and manufacturers of cosmetics and hygiene articles, a considerable number of soup cans, hams and bacon, flour packages, soaps, shampoos and toothpastes were found in the magazine. Often these goods were advertised through colourful illustrations of their

1.3 Advertisement for Campbell's Tomato Soup, originally reproduced in eye-catching scarlet. *Woman's Home Companion*, October 1923.

branded packages, but colour was also used for eye-catching illustrations of food products, such as hams, gelatine desserts and canned fruits
(see Figure 1.3).

In 1932 the use of colour decreased considerably; only 42 per cent of
the full-page ads contained colour in the March issue. Meanwhile, 54 per
cent employed black and white photography. To a certain extent this was
due to economic factors as photographs were cheaper than drawings or
paintings, but explanations can also be found in the developments within
photography. From the literal, matter-of-fact realism it had developed its
own artistic self-consciousness and begun to manipulate the subjects,
using extreme camera perspectives, variant focus, light and shadow, and
compositional juxtapositions to startle the eye or evoke a mood. Because
of this development, photography became more attractive to advertising
agencies and increasingly out-rivalled colour and modern art as a means
of arresting attention. Towards the end of the decade it saw a distinct
rise in popularity, which continued during the Depression. By early 1932
over 50 per cent of the advertising illustrations in a typical issue of the
Journal were photographs. The same year George Gallup confirmed the
merchandising prudence of the trend toward photography; his survey of
4,000 reader reactions ranked photographs as more effective than other
illustrations.[28] The advertisements in the *Companion* obviously followed
the trend.

While advertisers preferred, and obviously could afford, illustrations
in four colours throughout the 1920s, the magazine always made more
use of illustrations printed in one or two colours for its editorial material,
cover illustrations being the only exceptions. Of course, there may have
been economic reasons, but in the mix of new and familiar, the use of
illustrations in one or two colours also had its place, representing older
reproduction and printing techniques.

The relative increase of editorial illustrations in four colours was
negligible. During the period 1923–33, between 3 per cent and 6 per cent
of the magazines' pages contained four-colour reproductions for editorial
use. Quinan tried some on fashion and home decoration articles, but
concentrated them in the substantial amount of fiction – a strategy which
did not change much over time.[29] Editorial colour photographs were
rare exceptions throughout the period; one was tried in January 1930 on
an article with the significant title 'For Your China Cupboard – designs

that are both modernistic and old-timey in effect'. In May 1931 a colour photograph was used on an article on home decoration, but the issues of 1932 and 1933 that have been examined did not contain any editorial colour photographs at all.

Nevertheless, the use of colour for editorial material expanded. In October 1923 the art staff used colour for editorial material on 9 per cent of the magazine's pages. In March 1932 19 per cent of the pages contained editorial colour. But the great expansion occurred in the second half of 1932 and 1933; in November 1933, Quinan used colour on 44 per cent of the issue's pages. The increase mainly involved more one-colour printing. While no advertisements included one- or even two-colour reproductions in 1933, Quinan made use of single-colour printing in 33 of 128 pages in the October edition. This extensive use of single-colour printing was, just as in the case with colour photography, helped by the decision to print a larger part of the magazine using photogravure. And above all, it was typography and decorative elements in the layout that were given colour in this way (see Figure 1.4). The first letters in colour occurred in March 1932, when Quinan used coloured typography on 13.6 per cent of the magazine's pages, and the amount increased for each issue. This expansion of colour for editorial material also meant that colour occurred in the back pages as small illustrations, frames and vignettes.

The trend toward more colour did not come to a halt in 1933. From 1935 onwards editorial colour photographs began to appear regularly, advertisers introduced colour photographs that bled off to the edge of the page and colour photographs were taken across the binding.

Interpretation

The magazine's selling recipe can be described as a comfortable mix of 'new' and 'familiar' – a strategy that appealed to the *Companion*'s typical reader, helped it achieve large circulation numbers and attract advertisers. In this context editorial colour gradually increased in a harmonious coexistence with the magazine's large amount of full-page ads. When colour entered in to the typography and layout of editorial pages, the reading matter itself became 'stylish' in accordance with a new commercial aesthetic, which had been developed to meet the needs of business.

While magazines aiming at a more Europeanised upper class created

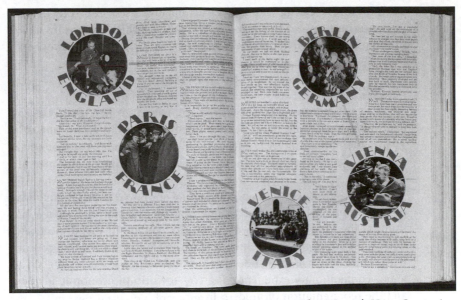

1.4 Article showing the use of colour typography, *Woman's Home Companion*, October 1933.

a sense of style and novelty through photography, modernist typography and what has been described as 'zig-zag' art, the *Companion* chose colour as the most important means to modernise its appearance in a specifically American context. Colour was an important ingredient in the new commercial aesthetic and by 1923 it had been applied as a method of creating a sense of 'style' and 'novelty' by a countless number of merchants aiming at the same market. In the mid-1920s manufacturers of goods exploited colour as never before. Many of these manufacturers, therefore, found an attractive medium for advertising in the *Companion*. In this way novelty was principally introduced through the ads, while editorial pages, which usually employed less colour, presented familiar topics. This mixture of conservative editorials balanced with modern advertising may be assumed to have facilitated the acceptance of the novelties represented in the advertisements.

Overall, the effort to modernise the magazine was constantly manifest in its design and editorial contents. As a commodity, this was essential for increasing sales and attracting advertisers. Aided by the new colour technology, reading matter itself became 'stylish', a 'novelty' underpinning the commercial aesthetic of American culture at this time.

Conclusion

From a European modernist perspective, magazines like the *Companion* and the *Journal* would never be celebrated for their design in contrast to their contemporaries, *Vogue* and *Vanity Fair*. However, a great amount of American women preferred these journals to magazines that aimed at a more 'Europeanised' reader.

As both the *Companion* and the *Journal* employed strategies that were highly consumer-led, we can assume that they actually reflected something of the taste of millions of American women. In this respect, such magazines are as worthy of attention as their more avant-garde counterparts. The *Companion* may indeed communicate just as interesting a story about contemporary experience, the construction of economic ideology and the representation of modern life.

Notes

1 The publishers of the *Woman's Home Companion* were S.L. and Frederick Thorpe (1873–81); E.B.Harvey and Frank S.Finn (1881–83); Mast, Crowell & Kirkpatrick (1883–99); Crowell and Kirkpatrick (1899–1901); Crowell Publishing (1902–39). It was produced in New York, Chicago and Springfield, Ohio (1896–1901) and in New York from 1901 until it ceased publication in 1957. The *Companion's* first known editor was J.F.Henderson (189–1902), followed by Arthur Vance (1902–07), Frederick L.Collins (1907–11) and Gertrude Battles Lane (1911–41).

2 J.Tebbel and M.E.Zuckerman (eds), *The Magazine in America 1741–1990* (New York: Oxford University Press, 1991), p.98.

3 See J.Scanon, *Inarticulate Longings, the Ladies' Home Journal, Gender, and the Promise of Consumer Culture* (New York: Routledge, 1995).

4 See Tebbel and Zuckerman (eds), *The Magazine in America*, p.98.

5 D.Reed, *The Popular Magazine in Britain and the United States 1880–1960* (London: The British Library, 1997), p.119.

6 Reed, *The Popular Magazine in Britain and the United States*, p.152.

7 See Tebbel and Zuckerman (eds), *The Magazine in America*, p.98.

8   Ibid.

9   Reed, *The Popular Magazine*, p. 124.

10 *Woman's Home Companion*, October 1923, p. 1.

11 C. P. Wilson, 'The Rhetoric of Consumption; Mass-Market Magazines and the Demise of the Gentle Reader 1880–1920' in R. W. Fox and T. J. Jackson Lears (eds), *The Culture of Consumption: Critical Essays in American History 1880–1980* (New York: Pantheon Press, 1983), p. 54.

12 *Woman's Home Companion*, November 1933, p. 4.

13 See W. Leach, *Land of Desire: Merchants, Power and the Rise of a New American Culture* (New York: Pantheon Books, 1993).

14 See, for instance, K. L. Endres and T. L. Lueck, *Women's Periodicals in the United States* (London: Greenwood Press, 1995), p. 170.

15 *Ladies' Home Journal*, February 1932, p. 3.

16 Ibid. The seven imperatives of the programme were: Maintain normal living conditions; satisfy your wants at today's prices; buy a home now; modernise and repair your home; join the parade to prosperity; stop being afraid; don't hoard your money – keep it safe.

17 *Woman's Home Companion*, November 1933, p. 4.

18 A large part consisted of full-page ads; in a typical issue of 1923, 30 per cent of the magazines pages and 64 per cent of the advertising space were full-page advertisements for consumer goods; in November 1933, 33 per cent of the magazine consisted of full-page ads, which constituted 63 per cent of the advertising space.

19 *Woman's Home Companion*, December 1925, p. 1.

20 See Leach, *Land of Desire*, 1993.

21 M. H. Bogart, *Artists, Advertising, and the Borders of Art* (Chicago and London: The University of Chicago Press, 1995), p. 22.

22 Ibid., p. 23.

23 Ibid., p. 23ff.

24 Quinlan's name and Art Director title appeared alongside Gertrude Lane's for the first time in April 1930. During the 1920s the title of Art Director gradually spread throughout the magazine industry.

25 Most often new features were introduced in advertisements and later followed in the design of editorial pages. While bleed-offs started to appear in the advertisements in 1935, they were not introduced for editorial material until 1939. The practice of allowing images to cross the binding, was also first introduced in advertisements (in 1932) but soon followed in editorial spreads.

26 R. Marchand, *Advertising the American Dream: Making Way for Modernity 1920–1940* (Berkeley, Los Angeles and London: University of California Press, 1986), p. 120.

27 Two four-colour illustrations for a story were presented on pp. 7–8 and two fashion plates in full colour were presented on pp. 27–28. The remaining 20 occurred between pp. 45–120 in 18 full-page ads, one page of illustrations of the children's department and a fashion plate. *Woman's Home Companion* 1923.

28 Marchand, *Advertising the American Dream*, p. 149.

29 Reed, *The Popular Magazine in Britain and the United States*, p. 159.

2 ✧ Fashioning graphics in the 1920s: typefaces, magazines and fashion

Jeremy Aynsley

T
YPOGRAPHY AND FASHION initially seem to be worlds apart. While typography is a design practice based on rules, principles, precision and economic prediction, fashion, it would seem, is a practice informed by breaking rules, intuition, style and fantasy – or so their stereotypes suggest. The aim of this essay is to explore moments from the history of design when overlaps and interconnections between fashion and typography can be detected. For although fashion history and graphic design history have tended to maintain their discrete paths, there have also been some significant instances when their boundaries have fruitfully crossed. Among the most obvious instances is the proliferation of graphic satire in eighteenth-century Britain, when fashionability and sartorial conventions were commented on in a vibrant print culture. This historical moment has been considered by a number of print and dress historians. Then there has been the interpretation of fashion magazines of the last twenty years, which scholars from a range of disciplines have analysed to reveal how fashion graphics can operate at sophisticated levels to convey attitudes towards style, identity and desire to particular audiences and readers. Work from this period is the product of an ever-increasing division of labour, with stylists, photographers, art directors, graphic designers and illustrators all part of the team acknowledged in the front pages of each issue.[1]

Interestingly, although sophisticated modes of analysis are available for the interpretation of graphic imagery, there are fewer apparent approaches for magazine and typographic layout that offer a historically contextualised reading of design decisions. This essay looks at the 1920s,

when graphic design for magazines was at an earlier stage of development – a period on which less has been written. Apart from compilations
of cover artwork, relatively little has been charted about the circumstances of magazine design, the exception being the profiles of key art
directors such as Alexey Brodovitch.[2] By contrast with such literature, this
essay deals more with the printed word than with the image, although
to separate them entirely is difficult. Specifically, it looks for connections
between the world of fashion and graphic design magazines by focusing
on the design of typefaces and considering their use in each context. I,
therefore, deal with the word – not as written, nor as a journalistic or
literary discourse, but simply as designed through type. In particular, I
am intrigued by the apparent absence of writing that connects fashion
and typography, either in that historical period or today.

A typeface called 'Fashion'

In 1929, the German designer Lucian Bernhard (1883–1972), by then
resident in New York, designed the typeface 'Fashion' for the American
Type Founders Company (ATF) (Figures 2.1 and 2.2). ATF was the most
highly regarded distributing company of type to printing houses in the
United States at that time and had recently become the sole source of
typefaces with a national network in the country. That a typeface should
be identified by this name signifies how typography and fashion were
intimately connected, at least, among certain design circles, and it, therefore, makes an intriguing starting point for this study.

   By the time the 'Fashion' typeface was introduced, Bernhard was
a prominent figure in the world of design. One of the first poster
designers originally associated with Jugendstil, he had defined a new
poster form, the *Sachplakat*, or object poster as it came to be known,
along with colleagues Julius Gipkens, Hans Rudi Erdt, Julius Klinger
and Paul Scheurich, principally for the printer Hollerbaum and Schmidt
in Berlin between 1907 and 1914.[3] A characteristic of this formula was
the equal assertion of object and brand in a simplified format. Interestingly, Bernhard was clearly attracted to methods of animating ordinary
objects through their commercial contexts. In the case of a poster for
the Stiller shoe company, for instance, the object is highlighted in a
particularly stylised way and isolated for the scrutiny of the customer or

2.1 and 2.2 Lucian Bernhard's 'Fashion' typeface, 1929.

reader, becoming a fashionable commodity with the additional allure of surface lighting through reference to photography. The addition of the singular company name made the poster international; brand and sign united in an effective and striking solution. Initially, Bernhard designed the letterforms for posters such as this and other commercial printing. Throughout his later career, he continued to produce either actual typefaces or display faces.

Within the wide range of products Bernhard depicted in his advertising campaigns, fashion remained a clear area of interest and expertise. The designer operated a studio in New York and Berlin throughout the 1920s – the practice was called Bernhard/Rosen – with Fritz Rosen remaining based in Berlin while Bernhard travelled frequently between the two cities.[4] On leaving Germany he had to adjust his approach to a different American market, which was not always straightforward for Bernhard. Roland Marchand has characterised American taste at this stage as more conservative in its preference for pictorial design solutions and dependence on extended copy-lines in advertisements rather than the

European tendency towards abstraction.[5] During periods when the studio could not raise sufficient graphic design commissions, Bernhard turned his hand to interior and furniture designs for well-to-do clients. He was, therefore, an all-round designer and in his commissions he was far from doctrinaire, his work revealing a variety of styles. This last characteristic marks Bernhard out from many other European designers of his and the next generation. While he was prepared to take steps to inflect his work with stylistic nuances, many younger designers were uncompromising in their approach to modern design and would not have felt comfortable tackling the range that Bernhard became involved with. At the time of the design of Fashion, Bernhard had been invited by Bruno Paul to take on the prestigious position of professor of graphic design at the Berlin Kunst Akademie by Bruno Paul. He was, in fact, barred for being Jewish and instead made the decision to settle permanently in New York, establishing a studio in the *New York Times* building.

As is the case for many typefaces, details of the exact circumstances of commission or circulation of Fashion are hard to find. Often the only way to gain a sense of the currency of a type design is to detect its use in the pages of editorial and advertising design in magazines and other forms of publication. To track the eventual currency of a particular type design is, therefore, inevitably a complex process – and I can only claim to have made a small inroad in this so far in the case of Fashion. To give an indication of scale of choice facing the art editor, designer or printer, by 1923, the catalogue of the American Type Founders Company contained 1,148 pages with what was available in the form of typefaces, display faces and ornament.[6] The repertoire of type designs was therefore vast, prompted by the change to mechanical composition through Monotype and Intertype systems during the previous thirty years, which made it easier for printers to offer variety of type for designs.

Fashion itself is a sans-serif typeface, otherwise known as Egyptian, or Gothic in America, a group of typefaces distinguished by the absence of terminal strokes associated with Roman alphabets. It fits well into the family of modern type designs of the late 1920s, a time of considerable shifts in attitude towards type in the western world. In McGraw's *American Metal Typefaces of the Twentieth Century*, it was described retrospectively as being a 'very delicate sans-serif, useful for fashion, advertising and social printing'[7] while a contemporary commentator placed it in 'a trio of delicate designs in which conventional form is well sacrificed to individuality'.[8] Where does this interest in delicacy derive and is it characteristic of a broader tendency?

In the 1920s the sans-serif typeface in general was interpreted as a modern design solution, associated with Constructivism and functionalism. Particularly in Europe, many new sans-serifs were designed at this time, when they were advocated as international and fulfilling the Zeitgeist, or the spirit of the age. The most orthodox examples of the sans-serif, however, were designed to fit the machine aesthetic of Modernism. These included Paul Renner's Futura of 1926–28 and Eric Gill's Gill Sans of the same period, with their evident references to geometrical sources. Both were attempts to provide industry standards in their respective countries of Germany and Britain. There followed a rash of other sans-serif typefaces in the late 1920s in Germany prompted by their commission from rival type-foundries. Some, such as Kabel (Cable) by Rudolf Koch of 1929, Beton (Concrete) by Heinrich Jost of 1930 and City by Georg Trump of 1931 signalled industrial or urban associations in their titles.[9] Fashion was, therefore, unusual in being cast with softer, decorative and possibly more feminine features. Apparently 'Fashion' was not so broadly taken up as another of Bernhard's type designs from the same time, Bernhard Gothic, which was celebrated in America as a good basic modern typeface and directly compared with parallel European designs. Indeed, according to Bastien and Freshwater, Bernhard Gothic was, 'One of the first contemporary American sans-serifs designed in 1929–30 designed … for ATF to counter the importation of the new European designs such as Futura and Kabel.'[10]

Fashion, by contrast, was a specialist typeface. In Modernist contexts of Europe, graphic design was considered as a form of industrial design – in partnership with the new architecture and burgeoning product design itself. Indeed, as is well known, the rhetoric surrounding the New Design concentrated on the metaphor of the engineer. In typographic circles, this position was epitomised by the figure of Jan Tschichold, whose book, *Die Neue Typographie* (*The New Typography*) of 1928 formed an important source of guidelines for the printer and designer.[11] The first stage of the book provided an art-historical context for the new typography, linking it to visual development in painting from Manet and Cézanne to Mondrian and Soviet Constructivism. Tschichold continued by discussing in detail principles of composition, from business letter-heads to what he characterised as 'the new book'. In the section on the design of magazines, Tschichold advocated the standardisation of actual formats of periodicals, as well as standard conventions of layout, column widths and type areas. He went on to recommend particular typefaces as suitable for the main body of magazine text, advised on bold or semi-bold sans-serifs for article headings, and illustrated his preferred arrangement of paragraphs and images with abstracted diagrams. This attention to all manner of print design was unprecedented in a Modernist context and Tschichold's advocacy was reflected in many contemporary publications, whether or not directly as a result of the book.

As a Modernist, Tschichold took the step of selecting a list of goods that he admired. In line with Le Corbusier's precedent, who a few years earlier had developed the concept of object types, Tschichold celebrated, 'electric light-bulbs, gramophone records, Van Heusen collars, Zeiss bookcases, tinned milk, telephones, office furniture, typewriters and Gillette razors'.[12] Collars are mentioned, for instance, because they could be interpreted as industrial forms and were standardised products. Tschichold argued that the final and purest shape of a product was always built up from geometric forms. Like others before him, and informed by Social Darwinism, he demonstrated a resistance towards the cycle of fashion and change. Therefore, as might be expected, we would be disappointed if we were to seek further connections between fashion and typefaces from Tschichold, or Modernist circles more generally.

It is possible to suggest that this absence or lack of articulation was in itself significant. In many respects, the discursive space of the new typography and architectural modernism overlapped, and within this, any inflection of style and the ephemeral was perceived as a problem. The latter, needless to say, were then important ingredients in the presentation of fashion, as they generally are today. As a symptom of this debate, the August 1930 issue of the German Werkbund journal *Die Form* is instructive.[13] A special number devoted to fashion, its lead article by Renate Richter Green, tellingly entitled 'Problems of fashion', considered rationalisation of dress. The author argued for the 'rational, elegant and beautiful dress'. Among other things, Richter Green advocated the transformation dress – one example was a multi-purpose garment with sleeves and other sections that could be added or taken away according to the occasion, and she went on to discuss fastenings and zips as modern elements which she perceived to be genuinely progressive. On the article's opening page, a Lee Miller photograph of a fashion model was straightforwardly juxtaposed with an eighteenth-century fashion plate to emphasise that to be of its time, each period needed its appropriate form of visual record.

Much has been written about architectural Modernism's difficulties with fashion by commentators such as Beatriz Colomina, Peter Wollen and Mark Wigley.[14] As Wigley has explored, architecture's struggle with fashion took the form of what he has called a 'pre-emptive defence that it was itself fashion'. He has written of architecture's 'identification of fashion with a generalised psychopathology of insecurity in the face of modernity'.[15] In a similar vein, Frederic Schwartz, writing about the German Werkbund, has shown how many of the design reformers, too, were ambivalent in the face of modernity. Attracted by the idea of instilling absolute qualities to objects, they sought industrial perfection, while trying to arrest the endless cycle of apparent waste in a system of constant renewal for which they blamed the fashion system.[16] Wigley, in his book, *White Walls – Designer Dresses: The Fashioning of Modern Architecture*, set out a series of contrasts between Modernism and modernity. To the Modernist, he attributed the values of the 'eternal truth, spirit, work, order, rigorous, erect, virginal, rational, standard, essential, honest, life, deep and internal'. Whereas modernity, he suggested, could be associated with the qualities of 'disorder, chaos, congestion, intoxication, play, dishonesty, illusion, weakness, sentimental, trivial, lies, prostitution, caprice, arbitrary, death, cosmetic, seduction, superficial, veneer, fake, substitute, superficiality'.[17]

Returning to the typeface 'Fashion', it was designed with idiosyncratic qualities which are in stylistic terms best characterised as *moderne* rather than Modernist. This contrast has been often invoked to define an alternative and, at times, oppositional impulse, identified with the luxury production of objects on display at the Paris 1925 Exposition Internationale Arts Décoratifs et Industriels Modernes.[18] The typeface is light, elegant and spatially generous. It has distinctive features that make it memorable – such as the low bars of the F, H, E, and so on. These, and the apparently upside down proportions of the S and the soft, Greek form of the E are distinctive peculiarities – as also the 'W', which is indebted to the letterforms of the Vienna Secession. Such an association, fully appropriate in this context, mark it out as fashionable or modish rather than purely functionalist. Its spatial airiness, emphasising the whiteness of the page both as unused space and the space taken up, enhances a sense of luxury and extravagance, conventional attributes of fashionable goods. Increasingly in the 1920s such white space connoted luxury on fashion pages. It was exactly such features that received criticism from some of the more doctrinaire modern typographers who would have seen them as, to use Wigley's terms, 'sentimental', 'cosmetic', 'capricious' or 'superficial'. Furthermore, it is possible to suggest that within typographic circles this disavowal of fashion reflected a false consciousness about fashionability parallel to that expressed in architecture.

Fashion and graphics periodicals

In design journalism of the 1920s, fashion graphics gradually became considered as a separate genre of the newly emergent graphic design profession. This can be appreciated if we take the graphics press and analyse how it represented the developments in fashion illustration and design for magazines. In these, the principal emphasis was on fashion illustration, with the majority of articles reviewing new styles and new figures – the standard gauge being Paris. Interestingly during my searches, I have found no articles from this time specifically dedicated to fashion typography, either on typefaces for use in fashion, or typography operating as a fashion system.

As an instance of this emergence, in 1925, the newly established German graphic design journal *Gebrauchsgraphik* devoted an entire issue to the field of graphics for fashion and textiles and its range is an indication of how the subject was being covered.[19] In an article by the editor H. K. Frenzel, 'On the Internationalism of Fashion Illustration', Frenzel moved from general characterisations of the industry to specific comments on the nature of illustration. He commented on the respective impact on fashion of the disappearance of national costume and speed of communications and transport. He concluded that France was the dominant country for women's fashion, while America was for menswear. Concerning the area of graphics he wrote: 'The style and direction of fashion illustration will always be international, just as fashion itself is. But just as there will always be individually gifted tailors who come forward, so too in Fashion Graphics, there will be people who stand out from the general style.' [20]

Consequently, in subsequent issues of the journal and other similar titles in the later 1920s and 1930s, such individual illustrators were profiled for their distinctiveness. One such was Reynaldo Luza, the New York based South American illustrator who was recognised for, 'his theme [is] the essential type of the modern *femme chic* and he has made her the charming motif of his magazine covers, deluxe catalogues and fashion plates'. [21]

What becomes interesting at this time is how equivalent in style and approach modern fashion and graphic design magazines were in terms of their general layout (Figure 2.3). It is easy to find parallels between their typographic arrangement of headlines, borders, body of text and general art direction. Symptomatic of this change was the revision of the conventional book-like layout of magazines to a more open, modernised, graphic

2.3 Layout of the graphic design journal *Gebrauchsgraphik* from February 1930 with an article on the fashion illustrator Reynaldo Luza.

layout. Both English and French *Vogue* changed typeface in the late 1920s to appear more modern, implying that typographic layout was becoming more worthy of attention – a general shift to active use of whiteness of the page, asymmetry of blocks of text, and use of more photography as illustrations. The magazine, for example, had wide borders, double column texts in modern Roman type and contemporary sans-serifs and display faces for headings; in fact, all close to Tschichold's prescription. The similarity between the two kinds of magazines was reinforced as advertisements by the same designers appeared in each. Often, these would be by high profile, prestigious designers with signature styles. It was commonplace for figures associated with fashion to work in other areas of graphic work. For instance, fashion illustrators made an impact on other areas of French and international advertising. Paul Iribe, the renowned illustrator, turned his hand to advertisements for the Paris printer Draeger Frères whose clients included Nicolas wines. Reynaldo Luza provided covers for *Harper's Bazaar* and also worked for Remington Rand Business Service Inc.; while again Draeger Frères supplied advertisements for publication in the American *Ladies' Home Journal*. Such crossovers led to a visual similarity and a shared sense of technical and aesthetic qualities between magazines that had previously been distinct fields of publishing.

It could be suggested that when considered as designed objects, fashion magazines of this time inhabited a curious space between the fashion modernity of France and the design Modernism of Germany. To explain, the infrastructure of the printing industry was highly dependent on companies that straddled the Atlantic – many foundries, printing machine manufactures and paper companies held offices in Germany and other parts of Central Europe and the USA. By contrast, fashion illustration had a different geography with Paris at its epicentre and radial points in London, Milan, New York and Berlin. Fashion drawing depended on the proximity between the fashion houses and the process of designing clothes and their representation, hence the pre-eminence of Paris at the time.

As one commentator wrote of work by Draeger Frères, 'The small, vivacious close-cropped head, the slender, waistless figure, the chic effect of utilitarian lines combined with feminine grace are noted here in a manner that is charming. This is a field in which the modern French type of design is unequalled.' [22]

Furthermore, it is possibly not too exaggerated to suggest that on the cover and interior pages of a fashion magazine these two traditions were culturally and metaphorically gendered – words as male and type, images as female and figurative.

This is all the more striking if we consider the other tradition of fashion illustration prevalent in the 1920s, which was more historicist in its sets of reference. In addition to the stripped mannequin heads of *moderne* illustration, Erté, Georges Le Pape and other illustrators important for the definition of an exclusive Parisian style, had developed a mode of illustration which was much more indebted to eighteenth-century precedents, having a lightness of touch reminiscent of copperplate fashion plates.[23] Without doubt, the basis of fashion illustration – the figure – posed a problem for Modernists, who in an ideal world would rather deal with abstraction than figuration. Frequently, the mannequin was made more acceptable to their aesthetic through simplification of drawn line, use of photography or Cubo-Futurist stylisation. As that same commentator noted,

> Fashion illustration is independent of the normal proportions. The everyday lines and shapes are not calculated to express it. What is necessary is, so to speak, a graceful exaggeration. The fashion artist is at liberty to make his creations incredibly tall and incredibly slim if by this means he can indicate more clearly the dominant mood of the moment. If we wish to fashion a clear-cut, well-groomed young man we make him so clear-cut that his features appear to have been sculptured with a chisel and sharpened with a razor. If his shoulders are to be square we make them squarer, and if the overcoat is full it must balloon about him.[24]

'Soyez à la Mode et employez Bifur'

By way of conclusion, it is interesting to turn to the French graphics magazine, *Arts et Métiers Graphiques* and return more specifically to the question of typeface design. This journal ran between 1928 and 1939 and had close associations with the fashion industry. The magazine took the form of a monthly review of all that was new in book design, typography and illustration with a strong emphasis on France. Many of its pages were devoted to the services that the publishing company itself, which also functioned as a type-foundry and specialist printer, could offer.[25] It was an example of a specialised trade publication aimed at a professional design and academic readership, international in profile.

For example, among such promotion, in 1929 an advertisement for typefaces available from Deberny et Peignot was published in *Arts et Métiers Graphiques*. 'Soyez à la Mode et employez Bifur' ('Be Fashionable and use Bifur') (Figure 2.4). The word 'Bref' – in short – adds to the telegram style of the advertisement as does the lack of any other decoration apart from the type elements themselves. The repeated word for 'fashion' was presented in all the typefaces available from the company at that

2.4 Advertisement 'Soyez à la Mode' from *Arts et Métiers Graphiques*, vol. 2, 1929.

point. The typefaces range from elegant Gothic, Shadowed, Egyptian and Roman to that at the bottom of the page, Bifur, which is a design of 1928 by A. M. Cassandre, the acclaimed French poster designer.

As if 'Soyez à la Mode' were not sufficient testimony to the interest of bringing together fashion and type, in the subsequent issues of *Arts et Métiers Graphiques* other advertisements appeared that drew together graphic novelty, technical advance and fashion references.

These appeared in further advertisements for the services of the photographic department attached to the company, who promoted the latest techniques of photo-collage. An announcement for their services in photographic and typographic setting, or TYPOPHOTO appeared, identified by the name given to the technique by the Bauhaus designer Laszlo Moholy-Nagy in the 1925 book *Painting Photography Film*.[26] The connection between the female model, a modern graphic layout, and notions of novelty and glamour were more akin to that frequently found in contemporary fashion spreads, or indeed even more advanced stylistically. Another announcement for the same department at Deberny et Peignot, depicted a subdivided portrait, one quarter solarised, a technique associated with Man Ray's fashion work (Figure 2.5). This was combined with overlaid typography and a delineated outline of the body and dress, presumably all presentational ideas targeted towards potential clients within the fashion publishing industry.

On the basis of revenue from staple typefaces, Charles Peignot, one of the company directors at Deberny et Peignot, embarked on greater artistic experiment by commissioning several modern typefaces. For this, he also turned to the designer Cassandre who eventually devised another two typefaces for the company Acier (1930) and Peignot (1937). The first, Bifur was the most distinctive, if not the most financially successful. It was much admired and incorporated in many designs of a *moderne* flavour, especially press advertisements in black and white for fashionable items. The individual letters of Bifur were reduced to geometrical forms with about half of each letter omitted and replaced by striking parallel lines. These gave the illusion of light and faceting, adding the jewelled effect of decorated metalwork, reinforced when it was advertised on silvered paper – all features associated with the Art Deco style. The character of the lettering was also adapted for architectural use on shop fronts. As one typographic commentator has noted,

French manufacturers went to great pains not to alienate their clientele
by presenting overly avant-garde concepts, but they could not simply
advertise such machine age wonders as furnaces, electrical items or Pyrex
pots and pans without introducing a degree of abstraction. Graphic for
industry, therefore, relied on Moderne styling to capture attention while
giving the consuming public a more-or-less clear image of the product,
designed to sell in the here and now.[27]

However, despite its distinctive *moderne* qualities, Cassandre himself
attributed startlingly Modernist credentials to his typeface, writing that
'Bifur was conceived in the same spirit as a vacuum cleaner or an internal
combustion engine', and that 'It is meant to answer a specific need, not

2.5 Advertisement
for Deberny-Peignot,
Paris, from *Arts et
Métiers Graphiques*,
vol. 3, 1930.

to be decorative. It is this functional character that makes it suitable for use in the contemporary world.' And he continued: 'Bifur was designed for advertising. It was designed for a word, a single word, a poster word.'[28] We are back in the world of Tschichold it would appear.

Cassandre's defensiveness about the possibility that the typeface could be interpreted as decorative betrays the full distorting force of modernist rhetoric. In another commentary from 1930, Cassandre made an interesting allusion to the relationship between the human body and the letter forms of Bifur. He wrote, 'In making Bifur we have not tried to make beautiful letters, but, on the contrary, without troubling about the letter itself, we have had to form a collection of simple, little, geometrical elements thanks to which the word is able to increase the power of its "image" considerably' and continued: 'If under these conditions Bifur is surprising on account of its unaccustomed aspect it is not because it is dressed in an eccentric manner but because it walks naked in an over-dressed crowd.'[29]

It is intriguing that the metaphor of dress and embodiment is used to explain the workings of typography. Such an association confirms that typefaces, like all other design forms, have the potential for associative as well as formal sets of references that connect with a wider social world.

The currency of Bifur is easier to trace than Bernhard's Fashion as it is such an instantly recognisable design. Immediately, it was a typeface taken up for use in the context of fashion. In the years that followed, Bifur became an internationally used typeface associated with women's interests. For example, Hans Schleger the German designer, often identified as Zéro, used it for Hudnut, the American cosmetic company, in a campaign run by Crawfords agency in Berlin.[30] In Britain, also for a branch of Crawfords, Terence and Betty Prentice employed Bifur in the redesign of Jaeger fashion house after 1929. And elsewhere, it was used as a source for, and spawned, several derivatives.

Conclusion

The separation of fashion and typography stems from a conflict between word and image which is well-grounded in many branches of western culture. In many respects, the word as printed traditionally requires a sequential, logical and abstract kind of comprehension, while the image depends on a holistic and concrete appreciation. Of course, type is also an aesthetic form and not simply functional; and therein lies the threat of contamination through decoration so strongly felt by Modernists. The desire shown by graphic designers to defend their fonts from accusations of fashionability and to design letters that reflected a Modernist agenda would appear to be partly a reaction to that perceived threat – to be solved by disassociating type and illustration. At this time, when the irrational power of the image as fashionable was on the rise, the call to pure reason and order was an attempt to arrest this anxiety, but it was equally a symptom of it.[31]

Bernhard's Fashion and Cassandre's Bifur are just two examples of typefaces from this period which offer new perspectives on the relationship between fashion and typography and their interconnectedness as they appeared on the pages of magazines. They coincide with a widespread and changing recognition of the power of typefaces prompted by developments in America. Advertising and marketing strategies were being analysed increasingly for their effectiveness, from the point of view of devices for selling and persuasion, rather than as pure aesthetic form. Perhaps this underlies the choice to brand typefaces with increasingly marketable names. A leading figure in French typographic circles, Maximilien Vox, who, incidentally, was also director of Le Service Typographique and adviser to Fonderies Deberny et Peignot, wrote, 'We live in wonderful times when advertising is just awakening to the startling discovery that it is not the picture which counts but the WORD. This is typography's coming of age.'[32] He continued, 'For a long time the copywriter's art had a highest degree of excellence in the United States and elsewhere with regard to the wording of the text, its credibility and vivacity, but the collaboration of the writer and the layout man is left to chance. My impression is that the time is coming when the text and layout will be the work of one man.'[33]

Underlying this comment was the awareness that American-style art direction was collapsing the boundaries between advertising and editorial approaches taken to magazines. Both Fashion and Bifur offered ways for a modern typeface to be noticed for itself when used in captions and headlines and were designed with associations with fashion to mark out their distinctiveness. In a broader sense, many of the experiments in typographic design of the 1920s, originating among the avant-garde, were formative for this recognition and fed directly into the increasing sophistication of graphic fashionability at this time.

Notes

A version of this chapter was given at the conference, The Fashioned Word, London College of Fashion, on 10 May 2002. I would like to thank Christopher Breward for this invitation.

1 For print culture in the eighteenth century, see D. Donald *The Age of Caricature: Satirical Prints in the Age of George III* (New Haven and London: Yale University Press for The Paul Mellon Centre for Studies in British Art, 1996); and M. Hallett, *The Spectacle of Difference: Graphic Satire in the Age of Hogarth* (New Haven and London: Yale University Press for The Paul Mellon Centre for Studies in British Art, 1999). For modern magazines and fashion, see S. Nixon, *Hard Looks: Masculinities, Spectatorship and Contemporary Consumption* (London: UCL Press, 1996); and P. Jobling, *Fashion Spreads: Word and Image in Fashion Photography since 1980* (Oxford: Berg, 1999).

2 A. Grundberg, *Alexey Brodovitch* (New York: Harry N. Abrams, 1989) and G. Baurent, *Alexey Brodovitch* (Paris: Éditions Assouline, 1999).

3 For the context of this poster movement see J. Aynsley, *Graphic Design in Germany, 1890–1945* (London: Thames & Hudson, 2000).

4 For a more detailed account of Lucian Bernhard see S. Heller, 'Lucian Bernhard: the master who couldn't draw straight', reprinted in S. Heller and G. Balance (eds), *Graphic Design History* (New York: Allworth Press, 2001).

5 R. Marchand, *Advertising the American Dream: Making way for Modernity 1920–1940* (Berkeley: University of California, 1985).

6 E. C. Kemble, *The Kemble Occasional*, October 1974, no. 12 (Edward C. Kemble, Collections on American Printing and Publishing, California Historical Society, San Francisco, 1974).

7 McGraw's *American Metal Typefaces of the Twentieth Century* (New Castle, Delaware: Oak Knoll, 1993).

8 A. Bastien and G. J. Freshwater, *Printing Types of the World* (London: Pitman and Sons, 1931), p. 145.

9 For an account of the context for these new sans-serif designs, see C. Burke, *Paul Renner: The Art of Typography* (London: Hyphen Press, 1998).

10 Bastien and Freshwater, *Printing Types of the World*.

11 J. Tschichold, *The New Typography: A Handbook for Modern Designers*, translated by R. McLean from *Die Neue Typographie*, 1928 (Berkeley: University of California Press, 1995).

12 Tschichold, *The New Typography*, p.10. Le Corbusier had argued for the identification of object types in the journal *L'Esprit Nouveau*. See also *Vers une Architecture*, Paris: Fréal, 1925: English translation F. Etchells, *Towards a New Architecture*, 1927 (London: Architectural Press, new edition, 1987) and *L'Art Décoratif d'Aujourd'hui* (Paris: Éditions Crès, 1925); English edition, *The Decorative Art of Today* (translation and introduction by J. Dunnett, London: Architectural Press, 1987).

13 *Die Form*, Berlin: H. Reckendorf, August 1930, vol. 5, no. 8.

14 B. Colomina, *Privacy and Publicity: Modern Architecture as Mass Media* (Cambridge, Mass. and London: MIT Press, 1994); M. Wigley, *White Walls, Designer Dresses: The Fashioning of Modern Architecture* (Cambridge, Mass. and London: MIT Press, 1995); P. Wollen in *Raiding the Icebox: Reflections on Twentieth Century Culture* (London: Verso, 1993).

15 Wigley, *White Walls, Designer Dresses*, p.39.

16 F. J. Schwartz, *The Werkbund: Design Theory and Mass Culture before the First World War* (London and New Haven: Yale University Press, 1996).

17 Wigley, *White Walls, Designer Dresses*, p.49.

18 See C. Benton, T. Benton and G. Wood, *Art Deco, 1910–1939* (London: V&A Publications, 2003).

19 *Gebrauchsgraphik, Monatsschrift zur Förderung künstlerische Reklame* (Berlin: Phönix Illustrations Druck Verlag, 1924–44).

20 H. K. Frenzel, 'Über die Internationalität der Mode-Illustration', in *Gebrauchsgraphik* (Berlin: Phönix, vol.1, no. 8), p.57.

21 M. Rathbone, '"La mode" interpreted by Reynaldo Luza', *Commercial Art*, vol. IX, 1930.

22 Anonymous, 'The Fashion Note in Advertising', *Commercial Art*, vol. VI, no. 35, May 1929.

23 The epitome of this would be Erté, see his book, *Things I Remember: An Autobiography* (London: Peter Owen, 1975).

24 M. Rathbone, 'La mode'.

25 *Arts et Métiers Graphiques*, Paris: Deberny-Peignot, nos 1–44, 1927–34.

26 L. Moholy-Nagy, *Malerei-Fotografie-Film*, Munich: Albert Langen, 1925, republished in translation as *Painting-Photography-Film* (London: Lund Humphries, 1969).

27 Steven Heller, *French Modern: Art Deco Graphic Design* (San Francisco: Chronicle Books, 1997), p.87.

28 Cassandre (Adolphe Mouron), 'Bifur, caractère de publicité dessiné par A. M. Cassandre', *Arts et Métiers Graphiques*, no.9, January 1929, p.578.

29 Cassandre, ibid. For a commentary see H.Mouron, *Cassandre: Posters, Typography, Stage Designs* (London: Thames & Hudson, 1985).

30 See P.Schleger, *Hans Schleger: A Life of Design* (London: Lund Humphries, 2001), pp.137–139.

31 I am indebted to Kate Forde for her observation.

32 M.Vox, *Commercial Art*, vol.VII, no. 38, August 1928.

33 M.Vox, ibid.

3 ✧ *Time Out* cover design, 1970–81

Emily King

DURING THE 1970s the covers of the London listings magazine *Time Out* occupied a significant role in the city's visual life. They were the wallpaper of a fast evolving urban culture and, even now, many of the young adults of the 1970s remember individual cover images. The look of the *Time Out* covers was derived from the confluence of necessity, technology, culture and the extraordinary skills of their designer, Pearce Marchbank. They reflect the absorption into the mainstream of 1960s underground culture, the masterful exploitation of photographic reproduction and the pressures of weekly, low-budget publication. 1970s *Time Out* represents a collision of technology and culture which created a spectacular visual impact.

Unlike British graphic design of the 1960s or of the 1980s, little has been written about the design of the 1970s.[1] The best way to explore this period is through interviews with the chief protagonists. This piece is founded on conversations I had with Marchbank, the most significant designer of *Time Out* during the 1970s, and with Tony Elliott, the magazine's founder and ongoing publisher in August 2001.

The underground press and *Time Out*

When it first emerged in 1968, *Time Out* was an annexe of London's thriving underground press. Tony Elliott, the magazine's founder, had been a student at Keele University when the two mainstays of underground publishing, *It* and *Oz*, were launched in 1966. Working on a student magazine called *Unit* (initially as advertising manager and later as editor), Elliott was keen to take part in this underground publishing event.[2] From 1967 on, he shifted the focus of *Unit* from local student activity to the largely London-based alternative arts scene, producing themed issues covering events or personalities allied with the underground.[3] The early *Time Out* grew directly from that magazine.

From the start, Elliott's ambitions extended well beyond Keele. The maximum number of magazines he could sell within the university was 300–400 and he believed he could circulate at least ten times that amount nationally. In mid-1968, Elliott printed several thousand copies of *Unit* and took them to London to try his luck. Once in the capital, Elliott became aware that there was room for a regular arts listings magazine. Initially he took the idea to editorial team at *It* magazine, which already published a small and somewhat sporadic listings section. According to David Robins, who was then working at *It*, the idea was 'poo-pooed', but Elliott and his then partner Robert Harris were not deterred.[4] After trying and failing to raise start-up capital from few other sources, Elliott borrowed a very small amount of money from family and friends. The first *Time Out*, a single sheet folded into an A5 format, was produced from Elliot's own front room in August 1968.

Later that year Elliott described *Time Out* to Richard Neville, the Australian founder and editor of *Oz* magazine. Neville was convinced that Elliot's venture would be lucrative and encouraged him to 'go out and get a Rolls Royce'.[5] In the long term Neville would be proved right, but he was being too hasty. *Time Out* was not a get-rich-quick scheme; instead it grew bit by bit, section by section. In September 1968 the magazine became an A5 booklet, by October advertisements began to appear, drawn from what Elliott describes as a 'self-contained economic community of natural advertisers' including small record labels such as Apple and later that year Elliott hired John Leaver, formerly of *Oz*, as advertising manager.[6] Over the same period, *Time Out* went from carrying partial listings, focusing on activity that was at the alternative end of the spectrum, to being a much more comprehensive entertainments magazine. This slow evolution culminated early in 1971 with *Time Out* becoming an A4 weekly publication. This is the form in which the magazine exists today.

After going weekly, *Time Out* went from strength to strength. The magazine developed new sections, hired more staff, attracted ever more advertising and eventually went full colour late in 1973. Concurrent with this success was the lingering extinction of the rest of the underground press, who yielded to oppositional forces from both without and within. Battering the underground press from the outside were the police and the legal system. From the late 1960s on, the premises of all underground papers (in 1969 eleven underground publications were registered with the Underground Press Syndicate[7]) were constantly subject to police raids. These raids culminated in 1971 with the prosecution of *Oz*'s editorial staff for obscenity and the jailing of three of its editorial staff.[8] Soon after this, the magazine went into liquidation. Around the same time, *It* had all but ceased publication. Likewise subject to police harassment, the publication was also torn apart by internal battles. While factions such as the Angry Brigade and the White Panthers promoted a more radical and violent path, newly organised feminists groups were beginning to make the publication's original agenda look dated and irrelevant.[9] By the mid-1970s, *It* was overcome by incoherence and inefficiency and in 1975 the publication appeared for the last time.[10]

Taking *Time Out* weekly

The plan to take *Time Out* weekly was hatched between Tony Elliott and designer Pearce Marchbank.[11] Marchbank was not the first designer to work at the magazine (after a brief period doing the design himself Tony Elliott had hired Paul Whitehead), but he was the first to have significant editorial ambitions. Before Marchbank joined *Time Out*, he had worked on *Friends* – an underground magazine that was created from the remnants of the British version of Rolling Stone after Mick Jagger withdrew his funding. At *Friends* Marchbank had come across Jon Goodchild, former designer of *Oz*, and it was Goodchild who established a connection between Elliott and Marchbank.

Marchbank was not typical of the designers who worked in the underground press. Unlike most of his colleagues, he had undergone a formal design education at Central School of Art, graduating with a first-class degree in 1969. At Central he encountered designers who pursued the more rigorous and intellectual strands of modernist design such as Richard Hollis and Anthony Froshaug and had been exposed to design influences both from Europe and the United States. Marchbank's design heroes were George Lois, the American designer of *Esquire* magazine known for his deft photographic covers and his condensed presentation of information, and Willy Fleckhaus, the designer of *Twen*, a German teen magazine celebrated for its idiosyncratic and adventurous design-led editorial.[12] *Esquire* and *Twen* were aimed at very different audiences, but common to them both was the marshalling of type and image in order to make a single, bold statement. The aim of Lois and Fleckhaus was to unify verbal and visual impact and, to that end, they aggressively cropped pictures and ruthlessly edited headlines.

While still at college, Marchbank had begun to design the magazine *Architectural Design* (*AD*) then located a short step away from Central in Russell Square. At *AD* Marchbank worked with design and production technology of the old school, using letterpress type and gravure illustrations. Marchbank's technological circumstances changed dramatically when he began to work for the underground press. When the high-profile British *Rolling Stone* mutated into the low-budget *Friends*, Marchbank began using some of the most innovative, cost-cutting techniques available. Calling *Friends* 'the first ever direct input magazine', Marchbank describes how journalists would type in their own copy on an IBM golf ball typewriter in house style (Times for text, Univers for captions) and he would literally cut and paste this copy into the layout.[13] In combination with the new, low-cost offset litho printing methods that had emerged in the mid-1960s, the IBM golf ball typewriter promoted a technologically primitive form of desktop publishing.

Set in the two typefaces available on the IBM golf ball, the style of *Friends* was noticeably more ordered than that of most underground publications. Arriving at *Time Out* in mid-1970s, Marchbank continued in the same vein. The magazine was professionally typeset, but Marchbank kept to a very restrained typographic palette, using Franklin Gothic for virtually all headlines and cover type. On the inside pages of *Time Out* Marchbank presented listings and editorial in a dense, information rich, but easily negotiable manner. Taking the magazine weekly, Marchbank carved out new sections from the fast expanding mass of listings. As such, a large part of Marchbank's design work overlapped with editorial functions. Among the new sections created at this time was 'fringe theatre'. This category was particularly significant as it was the emergence of low-budget, often politically motivated theatre in London, a form described by Robert Hewison as the 'natural force of expression for the underground', that had inspired the magazine in the first place.[14]

Time Out went weekly against a background of stiff competition from a new rival publication called *Ink*. The aim of both *Ink* and *Time Out* was to build commercial success on late-1960s underground culture, but while *Ink* attempted (and failed) to achieve this goal in one fell swoop, *Time Out* went about the task with stealth.[15] Through the 1970s *Time Out* shared increasing numbers of writers, illustrators and photographers with the mainstream press and expanded its coverage of mainstream culture, but all the while the magazine kept up the appearance of the credible voice of underground culture.[16] Members of London's underground may have been nonplussed by Elliott's businesslike manner (they described him variously as a 'suburban lad', a 'small shopkeeper', a 'straight-up Tory' and a 'soft-edged capitalist'), but most felt he was providing an extremely useful service.[17]

The strike

This was to change; *Time Out* was not able to strike a balance between commerce and the underground forever. When Marchbank joined *Time Out* in 1969, he brought with him a number of committed left-wing journalists, writers such as Duncan Campbell, John Lloyd and John Fordham, all former *Friends* writers. A decade later the *Time Out* newsroom was still staffed with the same leftist journalists and vehement anti-management stance was brewing. Things bubbled over in 1981 when Elliott attempted to dismantle the magazine's equal wage policy. This policy, whereby everyone from janitors to editors received the same salary, had been in force since the launch of *Time Out* and, although dear to the staff, Elliott believed that it had begun to stymie that magazine's growth.[18]

In response to Elliott's moves toward disparate pay, the newsroom held a strike that took *Time Out* off the streets for over four months. The magazine returned but the larger part of the staff had left, many going to work on the newly launched, politically-left, GLC-supported *City Limits*. Marchbank, meanwhile, had joined Richard Branson to design his new high-budget competitor *Event*. Within a few years *Time Out* was able to see off both of these rivals, but by that point it had become a PR-led, entertainments magazine.

Cover design: 1971–81

In the ten years between the launch of the weekly *Time Out* and the strike, the magazine achieved a considerable presence in London. The magazine reflected the concerns of younger, aspirant, politically conscious city dwellers, and it successfully communicated that agenda through its consistently eye-catching and succinct covers. Marchbank designed by far the greater proportion of these covers – 400 in the period 1971–1981. In the early years, the major considerations in the design of these covers were time and budget. The cover was usually created overnight before the magazine went to press and Marchbank had to derive a range of imaginative strategies in order to create original cover images in the face of extreme limitations. Using supplied photography, staged photography, illustration, collage and typography, Marchbank created a series of covers that captured the spirit of the times. Discussing the *Time Out* of the 1970s, the first thing most people remember are the 'brilliant covers'.[19]

The logo

As a student, Marchbank had become interested in the interaction between photographic processes and type. As part of his degree project, he had designed a typeface for photosetting that achieved different weights – light, medium and bold – according to the length of photographic exposure. Rather than a bold edge, this face had a slightly indefinite outline that allowed it to slip slightly out of focus. Features such as a small notch carved from the crux of each inward pointing corner allowed this typeface to blur without losing its form.

Marchbank revisited the same territory a few years later when he designed the logo for *Time Out*. Creating two sets of slightly out-of-focus Franklin Gothic capitals, Marchbank reversed the smaller out of the core of the larger. Then he ran the resulting typographic halo through a half-tone screen, lending it the appearance of a gentle glow, suggestive of a radiant neon sign. Appropriate to a magazine that advertises major cultural events, the *Time Out* logo resembles a radiant neon sign. This version of the logo was intended to be a stopgap, but has so far lasted thirty years.

Technology

Marchbank's *Time Out* logo was a function of photosetting technology:
rather than being incidentally photographic, it was essentially so. As such
it is an accurate reflection of a certain strand of the designer's interests.
Extending well beyond the design of letterforms, Marchbank's involvement in all the photographic processes of graphic design was profound.
He believes himself to be the first graphic designer to house a process
camera in his studio, a significant purchase that *Time Out* intended to
fund through design work for ventures such as The Place, a new experimental theatre outfit located close to magazine's King's Cross offices.

Through the acquisition of the process camera Marchbank was able
to achieve direct control of the photographic processes that traditionally
came under the auspices of trained camera operatives. In doing so, his
activities overspilled what was then understood as the territory of graphic
design. Rather than employing photographers to create images and tech-
nicians to reproduce those photographs, Marchbank became involved in
all stages of the process. For Marchbank, photography was not an activity
separate from graphic design, it was simply another graphic tool; photographs were not integral images, but elements to be employed within
broader graphic compositions.

The 1970s process camera was a large, ungainly and expensive piece
of equipment.[20] Standing around 4 feet high it had to be housed in a
darkroom and fed with a variety of unpleasant chemicals. By partici-
pating in the workings of the process camera, Marchbank cast graphic
design as an intensely material activity, one that included the physical
manipulation of imagery and the mess and randomness of photographic
technologies. The essence of process camera technology is the use of
filters that transform photographic material into images that can be
reproduced using non-photographic printing techniques. These filters
can either create a line reproduction of a photographic image or they
can create a half-tone reproduction: where a line image represents the
original photographic surface with blocks of continuous colour, a half-
tone image mimics the continuous shading of the photograph with a
series of variously sized dots.

Marchbank did not use photographic processes simply to reproduce
photographic images; he employed them to create entirely new textures.

In effect, the light filtering techniques that had been invented in the mid-nineteenth century as a means of faithfully reproducing the photographic surface were now reinvented as a means of manipulating and distorting images.

Throughout his years at *Time Out*, Marchbank used the process camera to rework images, particularly bland or bad quality images, into cover material. One of the earliest covers of this kind was a blue-drenched representation of the Warhol muse Viva that appeared the week 27 May–3 June 1971. Using a technique called posterisation, which involved creating a number of line images of the same photograph at different levels of exposure and then laying them one on top of another, Marchbank reduced Viva to a set of dark and light blue shadows. With the *Time Out* logo rendered in white at the head of the page, the rest of the cover type was set to the right of Viva's image written in the same blue and white as that marking the contours of her face. The element that binds together type and imagery on this cover is colour. Written in a chunky modern-style italic, the first word of the cover text is Viva. Short and typographically striking, Viva's name was as iconic as her face; both etched in blue, the one becomes equivalent to the other.

Viva owed her celebrity to the shenanigans at Warhol's Factory and her independent image was largely a by-product of his project.[21] As such, it is appropriate that Marchbank doctored the Viva photograph in the way that he did. Marchbank's treatment of Viva's image owes a substantial debt to Warhol himself, who frequently used the techniques of mass reproduction with the aim of semi-obscuring photographic images. However, while Warhol employed the techniques of mass reproduction but for the most part sold his murky images as limited edition screen prints, Marchbank heightened the mass-reproduced look of his work and remained within the bounds of the conventional mass media. Both Warhol and Marchbank used the dirty photograph as a look, but Warhol's work took that look much further from a context that might be considered authentic.

Running a photograph through a half-tone or line filter is akin to draping it with a veil: it puts an audience at one remove from the image. To exaggerate the effects of the half-tone process is to emphasise an audience's removal from an image, to heighten its existence as an element of mass communication. With this aim in mind, Marchbank often used

custom-made, half-tone filters in order to signal the processes of reproduction. In the case of the cover image of soul singer Millie Jackson (*Time
Out*, 27 January–2 February 1978), Marchbank created a half-tone filter
that separated the photograph into unevenly shaped patches of colour,
so that the singer's face emerges from a speckled gloom. One reason for
using this technique was to make the best of a poor quality supplied
image but, budget constraints aside, the speckled half-tone became an
element of a meaningful type/image composition. Under the headline
'The last Soul singer?' the heavily shaded image poses Jackson as an
endangered species, a woman of integrity struggling against the forces
of commerce.

The designer as editor

Marchbank's role at *Time Out* was never that of the conventional magazine designer. When he arrived at the magazine he spent several months
reorganising staff and editorial sections and from then on, even after
he had moved out of the *Time Out* offices and his relationship with
the magazine went no further than freelance cover design, he took a
quasi-editorial role. The process of creating the cover involved sending
the near-finished copy of the cover story to the designer by Monday and
the designer responding with an image by Thursday. Elliott recalls that
Marchbank took an active role in selecting the story and queried many of
the editor's decisions, often sending articles back and asking if there was
anything better.[22] Marchbank argues that the editorial team at *Time Out*
often favoured the obvious cover image, whereas he always sought out
the unlikely. In one instance, Marchbank rejected Mick Jagger in favour
of a polluted canal.[23]

For a story on Britain's nuclear bunkers (*Time Out*, 21–27 March
1980), Marchbank used images of six identical buildings apparently
located around the British Isles, that were supposed to be the 'military's
last outposts'. Photographic texture was used to create a bogus sense of
narrative: a misty image could have been snatched in less than optimal
conditions out of a sense of urgency; a sepia-toned photograph suggests
retrieval from a hidden archive; and a well-composed, sunny picture
might have been lifted straight from the army's own promotional
brochures.

Marchbank claims to have taken some of these images on site, but admits to have created others through photographic collage. The article illustrated by this cover discussed the government's plans for self-preservation in the face of nuclear threat. Acknowledging an element of fakery, *Time Out* qualified its claim that these buildings are all military outposts with the line: '*Some* [my italics] of these innocent-looking bungalows hide the entrances to Britain's Regional Seats of Government.'

Stories such as these have obvious editorial value and it was often the case that Marchbank was given much less to work with. In some weeks the cover was used to create a story when nothing in the magazine's editorial had stood out. In such an instance, Marchbank created a staged cover jointly promoting the film *Life of Brian* (a Monty Python spoof of epic films about the life birth of Christ) and an exhibition of 1930s design at the London Hayward Gallery (9–15 November, 1979). The cover shows the unlikely combination of the actor Michael Palin dressed in first-century AD sackcloth clutching a 1930s Corbusier chair. Appearing by Palin's head is the line 'The smallest story ever told' and in the curve of the aluminium chair leg 'The greatest exhibition ever staged' (Figure 3.1).

Time Out and Edward Heath

Elliott is now somewhat embarrassed by the magazine's political stance in the 1970s. Writing it off as very much of its time, he has argued that, since then, life 'has become hugely more sophisticated'.[24] Whatever the arguments regarding the sophistication of traditionally defined political concern, Elliott is right that the mainstream political publication has become a thing of the past. The agenda espoused by *Time Out* in the early 1970s has been rent in two and while the socially liberal parts of that agenda – racial and sexual tolerance, a more frank discussion of issues such as drug-taking etc. – have been absorbed by the mainstream – the politically left element has all but disappeared. It could be argued that underground culture was a victim of its own success. It was appealing, people bought it, and as a result it has been reduced to an existence as a niche in the market.[25]

It wasn't always this way. A cluster of Marchbank's most political covers come from the months between February and April 1974. Over

3.1 *Time Out*,
no. 499, 9–15
November 1979.

these months Londoners were suffering from the aftermath of a power
workers' strike which had reduced the country to a three-day week. By
February, the British public were looking forward to the opportunity to
depose Edward Heath, the Conservative Prime Minister held responsible for the crises. In the first of a series of explicitly anti-Heath covers
(1–7 February 1974), Marchbank showed a mock-up of Heath standing
blindfolded and naked but for a pair of boxer shorts against a brick wall
strewn with bullet marks. To the left of Heath is a poster for a fictional
operatic production called 'Tanks for the Memories', a line which functions both as a caption and as part of the image.

This cover was connected to an article by Duncan Campbell concerning
an imaginary scenario in which Heath had been deposed by a coup, hence

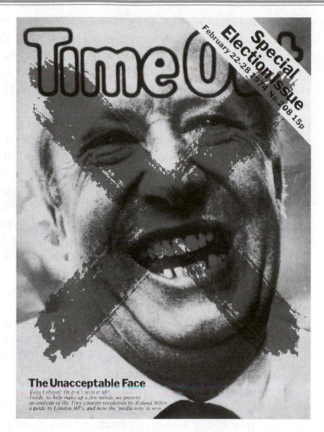

3.2 *Time Out,* no. 208, 22–28 February 1974.

The Unacceptable Face

the State Opera House in place of the Royal Opera House. In retrospect, Marchbank is not pleased with this composition, believing it to be too indirect to function as a cover. All the same, it does have qualities that make it interesting to compare with photomontages of an earlier era. In particular, as with the work of John Heartfield, it has a close relationship to 1930s photographic reportage in that it apes the grainy textures and grimy mise-en-scene of news photograph from that era.[26] But while these qualities were used by Heartfield to make his work appear current, they are employed by Marchbank to create a veneer of history.

A few weeks later and *Time Out's* political message was even more direct. During the week of election on 28 February 1974 (22–28 February 1974) the magazine ran a cover-size portrait of a laughing Heath with an

emphatic red cross over its centre. The headline read 'The Unacceptable
Face' and cover text began with the questions 'Vote Labour? Or don't
vote at all?' (Figure 3.2). The phrase 'the unacceptable face' was taken
from one of Heath's own speeches, a well-reported tirade against the
excesses of entrepreneurs, which singled out Tiny Rowland, the owner of
the African mining company Lonrho.[27] The image came from an agency
photograph of a relaxed, unguarded Heath. Marchbank cropped this
shot to emphasise unattractive qualities: Heath appears all double chins
and bad teeth. Using this combination of word and image, Marchbank
turned Heath's media presence on itself. The red cross over the centre of
the picture was drawn in crayon and enlarged many times to lend it a
roughness and a sense of urgency. This cross creates a stain across Heath's
face without obscuring his image. Representing the act of voting, the
mark is also a declaration of political intention on the part of *Time Out*.
By using red, the traditional colour of left-wing politics, the magazine
clearly allied itself to anti-Heath, anti-Tory politics.

On the last of the *Time Out* Heath covers, Marchbank faked a newspaper front page (19–25 April 1974). Using the headline 'Bloody Chaos',
the story behind this cover was the possibility that the entire crises of
the previous winter had been a government and press created concoc-
tion. To make this fictional newspaper look real, Marchbank ran the
text and image through a photographic filter to create the impression of
cheap print on low quality paper. The copy on this fake front page is an
ingenious parody of the language of crises – 'The worst Christmas since
the war … The end of western civilisation as we know it', but it relies on
photographically created textures for its full meaning. The months that
saw the demise of the Heath government mark the high tide of *Time
Out*'s involvement with the mainstream political process. Looking on
five years, to the week in which Margaret Thatcher was swept to power,
Time Out ran a single anti-Tory cover-story by Paul Foot titled 'An Election Nightmare'. This was the last time that an explicitly anti-government
message made the cover of the magazine.

Attracting a readership

The subject matter of *Time Out*'s Heath covers is specific to a time
and place, but their purpose – that of attracting a readership – is the

great universal of magazine design. With that in mind, Marchbank is particularly proud of the second cover in the series, the crossed-out Heath, which succeeds in being both direct and sophisticated at the same time.

Another *Time Out* cover that aimed to arrest readers was the VD cover of 1971 (25 June–1 July 1971). The image was a bright yellow VD printed large against a black background, relying on the mores of 1970s society for its impact. Sexually transmitted diseases were not a subject of polite conversation and the abbreviation VD (venereal disease) was shocking, even a little titillating, but also offered the rare promise of straightforward information about a fairly common condition: 'It doesn't take great odysseys of promiscuity to catch it' (Figure 3.3). That Marchbank was able to

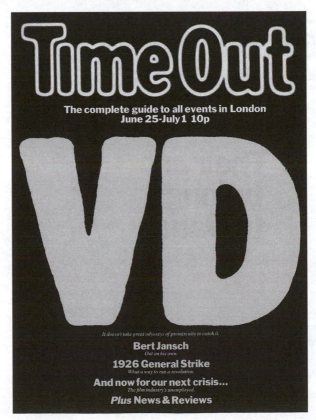

3.3 *Time Out,* no. 71, 25 June–1 July 1971.

use the same design formula again in 1979 (9–15 February 1979), this time printing a red VD against a white background, is a reflection of how little discussion of the disease had moved on over the decade.

Among the best known of all of Marchbank's designs for *Time Out* is the burning cover that was used to publicise the Arts Council's 'Dada and Surrealism Reviewed' exhibition at the Hayward Gallery in 1978.[28] Bearing the words 'Their art belongs to Dada' on a white background, this cover appears as if it is being consumed by flames. Beneath the charred remains of the cover, that week's contents page may be glimpsed. The production of this cover required a degree of design heroics. Usually the contents and letters page would be the last part of *Time Out* to go to press, but in this case it had to be put together several days in advance

3.4 *Time Out*, no. 406,
10–16 January 1978.

so Marchbank could use it as a prop. To make this possible, the design team reordered the format of the page, putting information that was already fixed at the foot of the page, the part that would be visible on the cover, and leaving the rest free for last-minute changes. The composition itself was created using photomontage; an image of a burning page, superimposed over the image of the contents page and printed with the headline and *Time Out* logo (Figure 3.4).

Alongside the twin strategies of attention grabbing and intrigue brewing, Marchbank used a third approach: straightforward seduction. Possibly the cover that best illustrates this approach is a 1971 portrait of Frank Zappa by the illustrator Peter Brooks (17–23 December 1971). In this image, Frank Zappa's face is traced in the notes of a musical score; dense patches of composition creating Zappa's trademark wild hair, beard and moustache. Inspired by the illustrations published in Massin's book *Letter and Image*, this cover was the idea of the illustrator himself.[29] Its coded form of portraiture is particularly appropriate to Zappa, an artist whose relationship with the media was never unambiguous.

Conclusion

Pearce Marchbank has described the later covers of *Time Out*, from the mid-1980s on, as a 'mush of faces'.[30] Obviously the former designer's judgement is partisan, but gathered together, side-by-side, *Time Out* issues of recent years create nothing like the variety and texture that they did twenty to thirty years ago. Growing up in South London in the 1970s my best friend's father, an animator working from a studio in Soho, pasted the covers of *Time Out* on the family's bathroom wall. As that gesture suggests, these covers provided the background to London life. *Time Out* has nothing like the same relevance today; it is very hard to imagine anyone preserving the magazine over the last decade.

In the period between 1971 and 1981, the covers of *Time Out* were editorial in their content. Their aim was to tell their audience something of interest and draw them in to find out more. In the British context this was something that subsequent magazines such as *City Limits*, *The Face* and *iD* continued in the 1980s, using graphic immediacy to signal a distinctive point of view to their readers.[31] Meanwhile, *Time Out* began to run the occasional consumer or mainstream entertainment cover, but they certainly did not dominate the magazine in the way that they do now. No longer a discursive space, the cover of today's *Time Out* is a purely promotional arena.

The single most important ingredient in the construction of the *Time Out* covers was speed. In the years that Marchbank worked on the magazine he was required to trawl through content and come up with a cover image in a matter of days, and sometimes hours. Under unrelenting time pressure, Marchbank's response to the content of the magazine was consistently forthright and imaginative. In his role as designer in the early days of *Time Out*, Marchbank gave shape to the content of the magazine and played an important role in determining its scope and tone of voice. Designing the covers as a freelance later in the 1970s, Marchbank continued to exert a decisive influence on the message of the magazine. Through that period, Marchbank's great achievement was to fuse design with editorial, thereby creating a hybrid with which he was able to command the attention of 1970s London.

Notes

1 The birth of British graphic design in the late 1950s and early 1960s is discussed at length in Rick Poynor's *Typographica*, an account of Herbert Spencer's magazine of the same name (London: Laurence King, 2001). The important figures from this era, designers such as Alan Fletcher, Bob Gill and Robert Brownjohn, have all been the frequent subjects of profiles in British and international magazines such as *Eye*, *Graphis*, *Print* and *Communication Arts*. Equally, the well-known designers of the 1980s, chiefly the triumvirate of Neville Brody, Peter Saville and Malcolm Garrett, have been the subject of monographs (*The Graphic Language of Neville Brody* (London: Thames & Hudson, 1988), *Designed by Peter Saville* (London: Frieze, 2003) and numerous articles in both the specialist and popular presses. A recent addition to the literature is Rick Poynor (ed.), *Communicate: Independent British Graphic Design since the Sixties* (London: Barbican Art Gallery and Laurence King, 2004).

2 Interview with Tony Elliott, London, 2 August 2001.

3 Ibid.

4 N. Fountain, *Underground: The London Alternative Press 1966–1974* (London: Routledge, 1988), p. 81.

5 J. Green, *Days in the Life: Voices from the English Underground 1961–1971* (London: Minerva, 1989), p. 262.

6 Elliott interview, 2 August 2001.

7 R.Hewison, *Too Much: Art and Society in the Sixties 1960–75* (London: Methuen, 1986), p.173.

8 For a first-person account of the *Oz* trial see R.Neville's *Hippie Hippie Shake* (London: Bloomsbury, 1995).

9 Fountain, *Underground*, p.154.

10 Ibid., p.193.

11 Pearce Marchbank gave me his perspective on the early days of *Time Out* in an interview at his studio in the Brunswick Centre on 7 August 2001.

12 *Twen* was launched in 1959 and both its style and content are attributable to its designer, Willy Fleckhaus (1925–83). The magazine was aimed at an audience of affluent young Germans and offered a mix of sex, pop, celebrity, mysticism and social affairs. Fleckhaus employed a number of pioneering photographers and illustrators including David Hamilton and Hans Hillman.

13 Marchbank interview, 7 August 2001.

14 Hewison, *Too Much*, p.189.

15 For an account of the ill-fated *Ink* see Green, *Days in the Life*, pp.370–372.

16 Ibid., p.264.

17 Ibid., pp.262–265.

18 *The London Programme*, ITV, October 1981.

19 Green, *Days in the Life*, p.264.

20 In the late 1980s Pearce Marchbank paid around £4,000 for his last process camera. By the early 1990s he found himself paying £10 to have someone take it away.

21 Founded on New York's East Side in 1962, Andy Warhol's Factory evolved into a unique combination of professional and social space. It also spawned its own set of mini-celebrities, the fates of whom are chronicled at www. warholstars.org.

22 Elliott interview, 2 August 2001.

23 Marchbank interview, 7 August 2001. Another of his less obvious cover stories was the scandal surrounding the cost of planning the new town of Milton Keynes (22–28 October 1971) which showed a sign to Milton Keynes and the headline: 'This sign cost £17,000,000'.

24 Elliott interview, 2 August 2001.

25 The decline of the traditional left wing is the subject of Jonathan Coe's novel *The Rotter's Club* (Middlesex: Viking, 2001). Told from the perspective of four teenage protagonists, Coe's story incorporates the failing power of

the unions and the rise of Thatcherism, the progress of sexual and cultural permissiveness, and the considerable impact of punk on late-1970s popular culture.

26 For an account of the work of John Heartfield see *John Heartfield: 1930–38* (London: Art Data, 1992).

27 Nearly a decade later, in 1983, Tiny Rowland bought the British newspaper *The Observer*. Adopting the role of chairman, the purchase gave Rowland a position from which to counter further unfavourable media representation.

28 'Dada and Surrealism Reviewed' was curated by Dawn Ades and showed at the Hayward Gallery in London from 11 January to 27 March 1978.

29 Massin, *Letter and Image* (London: Studio Vista, 1970). See in particular Marshall Foch's portrait of Georges Teherukine, first published in the *Pantheon of Glories*, 1930.

30 Marchbank interview, 7 August 2001.

31 R. Poynor (ed.), *Communicate* (2004), pp. 48–75.

Part II
Magazines and the consumer

One of the strengths of design history's recent emphasis on the consumption of magazines has been its challenge to the idea of a generic middle-class market. The first essay in this part, for instance, argues for a nuanced approach towards historical consumers, and one that more accurately reflects their diversity. Magazine advertising is conceived as just one element of a visual language that by 1900 was teeming with posters, plaques, leaflets and handbills. In this context, and particularly in relation to an inexpensive commodity like soap, the promotional culture of everyday life becomes an active experience for all but society's poorest. The second essay again addresses the relationship between magazines and the female reader, in the case of a series of 1950s articles from *Woman*. This popular British consumer magazine promoted modern design in a series of profiles of new homemakers. A study of the editorial position suggests that the magazine adjusted and adapted notions of good taste to meet its readers' interests, allowing for a broader and more socially representative view of modern life. By contrast, the third essay focuses on the exclusionary power of 1960s fashion photography which targeted white readers through its fastidious construction of 'blackness'. Applying cultural and sociological theories, the author unmasks the latent ideological meanings in such images. This political reading of magazines reveals much about contemporary attitudes towards those who were considered exempt from the market, as well as those who were identified with it.

4 ✧ 'The All-Conquering Advertiser'? magazines, advertising and the consumer, 1880–1914

Victoria Kelley

Class-barriers have fallen before the all-conquering advertiser. Whether we are poor, and buy our halfpenny Imperialist daily, or rich, and read our sixpenny Socialist weekly … we are favoured with the same solicitous regard and flattering assurance as to the value of our custom in the economic world.[1]

B Y THE OUTBREAK of the First World War, advertising had become of central importance to the periodical press, with magazines and newspapers in which advertisements were prominent reaching rich and poor alike. Advertisements contribute an important element to the material character of the magazine; we cannot consider the magazine as an object without taking note of advertising, or properly account for how the magazine interacts with its consumers without exploring how readers respond to advertisements as well as editorial matter.

This essay concentrates on the relationship between the magazine, the magazine advertisement and the consumer during the period 1880–1914. Much work on historical advertising has concentrated on the advertisements themselves, rather than trying to imagine how they would have been received by their consumers. Studies that have attempted a 'reading' of advertisements have used a semiotic approach, which draws most or all of its evidence from the text and image of the advertisements alone. Examples of this sort of approach include Thomas Richards's *The Commodity Culture of Victorian England*. Richards constructs a bravura and extremely stimulating analysis of Victorian commercial imagery, seen as an integral part of a culture of spectacle, but perhaps falls into a trap identified by Jonathan Rose: 'Critics repeatedly commit what might be called the receptive fallacy: they try to discern the messages a text transmits to an audience by examining the text rather than the audience.'[2] In a similar vein is Lori Anne Loeb's *Consuming Angels: advertising and Victorian women.* Loeb sources many of her advertisements from the John Johnson Ephemera Collection at the Bodleian Library in Oxford. The use of such uncontextualised material throws into particularly sharp focus issues of readership, and the potentially acute danger of hypothesising from images to an imagined consumer who we really know nothing about.

This study introduces primary sources produced by the advertising industry itself: the 'all-conquering advertiser' cited at the opening of this essay features in a business guide to advertising which is representative of a growing body of literature produced by a fast-developing industry from the last decades of the nineteenth century onwards. Such sources, with all their consistencies and inconsistencies, inclusions and omissions, are a rich source of information produced by the advertising agents who created the advertisements. If we are to 'read' images like the soap advertising featured here, to interpret them as historical evidence, we need to understand the images themselves, but also to understand their complex *contexts*. It is here that advertising industry sources can contribute, alongside a sensitive awareness of relevant social and cultural factors. What messages did the advertisers who produced such advertisements think they were communicating, and how did they understand the techniques available to them? What did they think about their audience or audiences?

This essay's focus is largely contextual and methodological, as it has arisen from problems encountered in sampling and *interpreting* advertisements from magazines.[3] The goal is to establish some technical information about the nature and functioning of such advertisements. A detailed examination of such matters may suggest how appropriate and sensitive use of advertisements as source material can allow the historian to begin to understand the advertisements themselves, their relationship to the magazines in which they were printed, and the historical consumer, in particular often overlooked groups such as working-class consumers. Richards and Loeb concentrate exclusively on the middle classes. However, Lady Bell, who surveyed the reading matter of Middlesbrough ironworkers in 1907, found that these members of the working classes at least frequently read a wide range of periodicals, including weekly family newspapers and penny magazines, which may have included women's penny weeklies.[4]

The issue of class becomes a pressing one: were there particular products which were advertised to particular classes, genders or demographic groups? Were some products advertised in different ways to different groups of consumers? Do the pages of, for instance, mass-market periodicals, yield up different advertisements, for different products, or indeed different advertisements for the same products, when compared to upper-class ladies' periodicals? And how did press advertising relate to other sorts of advertising, if we think about the totality of commercial messages which consumers may have been subjected to? In order to answer these questions we really need to get *directly* to the historical consumer. This difficult task is certainly not for this short chapter:[5] however, we can, through advertising industry sources, get to the historical advertiser who is only one step removed from the consumer he addresses.[6]

The first section briefly outlines the changes in periodical publishing of the 1880s onwards which saw advertising become an integral part of a new popular press. The second section introduces advertising industry sources, allying analysis of these to examples of advertisements taken from the pages of women's and popular periodicals of the period. This is followed by a third section which offers a suggested 'reading', or rather several readings, of one particular advertisement. All of the advertisements studied are for a single product, soap, which was one of the most heavily advertised commodities from the 1880s through to 1914. It was a mundane and inexpensive item which was nevertheless weighed down and puffed up by numerous ideological associations which linked it variously with purity, rectitude and moral probity, with hygiene and protection against the invisible monsters of disease germs, and with vanity and luxury. Toilet soap, household soap, laundry soap, soap flakes and soap powders were advertised steadily and heavily. Even a cursory reading of magazines from the period is sure to turn up plenty of examples of advertisements for Sunlight soap, Pears' soap or Watson's Matchless Cleanser, to cite just three common brands, making soap advertising rich subject matter for an examination of advertising practice in this period.

The emergence of a mass press

There is a considerable literature on the popular magazines, and especially the women's magazines, of the late nineteenth and early twentieth centuries.[7] The work of Ballaster et al. and Beetham, gives due prominence to the importance of considering advertising in any analysis of such magazines, noting that advertising's messages are especially important to the overall picture in women's magazines.[8] Here readers were traditionally constituted *as consumers* by their very gender, and advertisements 'made explicit ... the link between femininity and consumption (represented as "shopping")'.[9] Gender is an ever-present matter in considering the relationship between the consumer and the advertisement in the pages of the magazine; this is especially the case when looking at the product which furnishes the examples on which this paper is based – soap.

The 1890s was a crucial period of change, when the rapid development of a truly popular press saw the birth of new magazines and newspapers which kept their cover price low by selling large amounts of advertising space.[10] The expansion of the press to appeal to the working classes, and the expansion of the role of advertising within the press, were both part of the same process, whereby advertising revenue subsidised cover price, encouraging a broad readership, which in turn attracted advertisers. The *Daily Mail* (first published in 1896) is usually cited as the daily newspaper which first reached a mass audience,[11] and amongst magazines it is women's periodicals which have received most attention from historians. Prominent women's titles of the period included the new penny weeklies such as *Forget-Me-Not* (1891), *Home Notes* (1894) and *Home Chat* (1895), which all offered a mixture of domestic advice, society gossip, fashion hints and fiction in a cheap, chatty and friendly format, with plenty of illustrations and lots of advertisements.[12] Weekly family newspapers such as *Reynolds's Newspaper* and *Lloyd's Weekly Newspaper* (both specifically cited by Lady Bell in her description of the reading matter of Middlesbrough ironworkers) blended radical politics with sensational reports of crime and scandal, and here too the change in the 1890s is notable. These long-established working-class newspapers began to include more and more advertisements, of increasing graphic sophistication, from around 1897 onwards.[13] Before the 1890s, advertising revenue had been a supplement to the cover price; now it became the backbone of periodical finances. A similar development occurred in the United States at the same date as, 'publishers made a definitive shift – from selling magazines directly to readers to selling their readership to advertisers'.[14]

As more advertising space was sold, advertisements themselves changed, becoming larger, more visually attractive, and more sophisticated in their messages. The cause of this change was not just altered magazine finances, and improvements in reprographic technology,[15] but also wider economic developments: this was the period when the commodification of many household goods was in full swing, with manufacturers developing branded and packaged products which they advertised aggressively. The pages of the new popular magazines of the 1890s became an important site for such advertising, and connections began to be made between editorial matter and advertising, as advertisements were juxtaposed with, for instance, related advice columns.[16] Advertisements grew in number, spilling out of their traditional place at the start and end of the periodical, flooding onto pages interleaved between articles and features, and invading the editorial pages themselves, seeping in from the margins. This tendency was most pronounced in periodicals aimed at the lower end of the market – the family newspapers such as *Reynolds's* and *Lloyd's*, and the cheap informal women's penny weeklies founded in the 1890s. Advertisers were certainly beginning to be aware of the potential of the working-class market.[17]

Agencies and the developing art of advertising

As the popular press and press advertising grew in scope and sophistication, advertising agencies began to emerge from press agencies.[18] The latter were simply space-brokers, handling the placing of fairly basic publicity material in a range of periodicals. However by the late nineteenth century they were becoming organisations which could also write copy, produce illustrations, and orchestrate what were beginning to be called 'campaigns', offering advertisers expertise in a newly-developing

industry. By 1914 one industry source could claim that the 'modern up-
to-date agency' would handle every stage of the advertising process, from
giving a product its name through to checking that posters were in the
sites paid for, and every job in between: 'in short, the agency will advise
and co-operate with the advertiser at every turn and relieve him of every
detail of his publicity'.[19]

The growing advertising agencies published press directories which
started as simple listings. These provided basic information for advertisers on a huge range of newspapers and magazines, dealing with such
matters as frequency of publication, cover price and advertising rates. By
the 1890s some of the larger agencies prefaced the listings with extensive
material on the art and business of advertising, including reviews of
the past year's notable campaigns, and examples of successful advertisements.[20] In addition, business manuals began to appear on 'how to'
advertise, becoming especially common after around 1900 as advertising
agents sought to establish their business as a modern profession. It is
to these advertising industry sources that we can turn for a contemporary eye on advertising practice. Richards actively rejects these sources,
playing down the role of individual advertising agents and preferring to
see Victorian advertising as vigorously amorphous – an extremely active
body with no head.[21] This essay gives advertising industry sources a little
more credit – if we are content to use the images which professional
advertisers produced as historical evidence, we should also be prepared
to take on board what those advertisers *say* about those images.

One of the strongest messages to emerge from a reading of advertising industry sources is that advertisers of the day were well aware of a
range of different media. All the directories and business manuals follow
the same categories, dividing advertising into three branches; 'press',
'outdoor', and 'direct to the person'. One cannot, when looking at advertisements in magazines, consider such images in isolation – for most
consumers, the commercial imagery they saw on the pages of their daily
newspaper or weekly or monthly magazine would have been just part of
the totality of advertising material they were exposed to. One advertising
industry source, writing in 1914, weighs up the relative merits of press
and poster advertising thus:

> The newspaper advertisement can appropriately be used to educate the
> public by explanation and argument, while the poster, speaking to men

and women as they hurry to and fro, serves rather to announce and remind and thus to supplement the influence of the arguments in the press.[22]

Advertising agency Mather & Crowther notes the highly visible presence of advertising images on public transport, indicating the ubiquity of the advertisement in very many sites in the urban environment: 'London omnibuses and trams are indeed covered very abundantly with Advertisements of every kind, inside and out, on the steps, on the backs of the chairs, and everywhere where an announcement can be seen.'[23]

Work on the urban geography of the Victorian and Edwardian city suggests how people of different classes and different genders occupied the streets in different ways.[24] It would be useful to apply this research to the matter of outdoor advertising, to assess in greater detail how posters etc. would have been viewed by their audiences. Even without detailed consideration of such issues, it seems clear that we are dealing here with a complex topography of messages, media and audiences within the public spaces of the city, interacting with those images seen on the pages of magazines.

The second point to emerge from advertising industry sources regards the audience reached by all those advertisements in magazines and newspapers, on hoardings, trams and omnibuses and stuffed through the letterboxes of countless homes. Richards and Loeb, as has already been noted, concentrate on the middle classes, but the advertising agency directories and the business manuals take a more democratic view. They are very clear that advertising's reach was wide, and becoming wider. In the first place, the press itself appealed to a mass readership: 'There is, in fact, no class of consumers which cannot be affected through the medium of some section or other of the Press.'[25]

And while press advertising relied on consumers actively buying and reading a magazine or newspaper, other forms of advertising were unavoidable to anyone who simply walked down the street – 'out-door advertisement forces itself upon the attention of all, willy-nilly'.[26] Some manufacturers used the streets as a stage for spectacular publicity stunts to advertise their products. *Deacon's Newspaper Handbook* describes an elaborate procession of a carriage and twelve liveried men distributing free samples of Hudson's soap,[27] and W. H. Lever, head of Lever Brothers, the makers of Sunlight soap, describes a similar procession by another soap manufacturer, distributing prizes in one of the wrapper schemes which were so common in the soap business, especially in the 1890s.[28]

An advertisement for Cuticura soap from April 1895 ran in *Myra's Journal*,[29] however it also appeared in a number of other periodicals, namely the *Queen* and *Reynolds's News*.[30] While *Myra's* was a monthly fashion magazine, aimed at lower-middle class women,[31] the *Queen* was a lavish and high-quality 'ladies' illustrated newspaper',[32] costing sixpence weekly and aimed at the 'upper ten-thousand' of British society.[33] *Reynolds's News*, by contrast, was a family Sunday newspaper which sold to the working classes, such as the ironworkers and their families surveyed by Lady Bell, at a penny.[34] Here is an example of a product which is advertised across class barriers, using the same language (in this case an appeal to maternal/parental instinct mediated through the rather jolly figure of a trusted family doctor) to speak to consumers of vastly differing means and situations. There are plenty of other instances of advertisements which were placed in a wide range of periodicals, see for instance the advertisement for Lifebuoy soap in Figure 4.1.

In shops too, advertising images proliferated.[35] Even a cursory look at photographs of shop windows or interiors from the period proves how ubiquitous showcards and posters were becoming. In all but the very poorest districts, buyers would have seen such promotional imagery as they went about their daily grocery shopping. Even those people who never read a newspaper or magazine may well have seen the same advertising images that the press carried. Mather & Crowther in 1895 state that many of their customers used the designs drawn up for press advertisements to produce additional colour 'Show Cards, Counter Cards, Leaflets etc.' which would then have been displayed in shops and shop windows, and perhaps distributed house to house.[36]

Thus when we think about advertising in the 1890s or 1900s, we should not just imagine a middle-class audience receiving or resisting the brand-names, slogans and images. Increasingly, a good proportion of the working classes too were passive, or active participants in what Richards calls 'the system of advertised spectacle'.[37]

Advertisers were of course aware that some products and some media reached much more defined groups of consumers in terms of class, region and, most significantly, gender.[38] On this issue, the consensus

4.1 Advertisement for Lifebuoy soap (*Home Chat*, 4 February 1905, p. 325). This advertisement was also shown in the *Queen* (21 January 1905, unnumbered page). The design, layout and copy are almost identical, but the *Home Chat* version is a simplified version for lower quality reproduction.

seemed to be that women were more inclined to respond to illustrations and narrative, men to text and 'fact', but that the female consumer was nevertheless a shrewd judge of the goods she bought:

> She is, in most things, a keener and quicker observer than man. She, moreover, demands in detail a description of the goods she is asked to buy, as often as not requiring that particulars as to cost shall be set out in an advertisement.[39]

However, with the exception of gender, it is not always easy to pick out an awareness of such differences between consumers from the advertisements themselves. By the 1890s, a mass market for advertised goods was indeed emerging. We should not overstate this point; for many people in the lower reaches of the working classes daily existence was still a struggle for subsistence and could not have included many 'consumer' choices; those who were slightly better off engaged with consumer goods through a limited number of relatively cheap and humble articles. Nevertheless, that engagement was there; many advertising industry sources make mention of a class of products which are affordable to, and purchased by, a mass market – these items of 'universal demand' or 'universal consumption' include soap, which is often cited as an example.[40] To return once more to the example of Cuticura soap, this was a product which was advertised in the same way to very diverse consumers, but the immediate context of the advertisement on the page in different periodicals may have altered its reception, as meaning was constructed by juxtaposition and intertextuality (was it positioned next to an advice column, beauty hints, or other advertisements for similar or very different products?).

A further notable characteristic of the big advertisers, whether they were pushing soap, baby food or corsets, was the *variety* of approaches taken. When looking at historical advertising, it is tempting to look for modern-day techniques, such as tight brand management, but in the late nineteenth and early twentieth centuries the brand was in its infancy and was certainly not presented with the same ruthless single-mindedness of message that is common today. Pears' campaign, using the slogan 'Good Morning, have you used Pears' soap?' was repeated with a bewildering array of characters, images, graphic styles and copy throughout the entire period under discussion.[41] Overlapping with it were at least two other 'campaigns', one which used celebrity endorsements in the 1880s, and a second which stressed Pears' good value for money in the 1910s (Figure 4.2). These approaches can be seen in close temporal proximity in the pages of the *Queen*, *Myra's Journal*, *Home Chat*, and *Mother and Home* (another cheap mass-market women's weekly). And alongside these groups or series of advertisements which formed identifiable campaigns were individual images, which likewise could appear and reappear over long periods. The famous 'Bubbles' advertisement, based on a painting by John Everett Millais, was first used in the late 1880s, and was still being reproduced as late as 1915.[42] This use of images and slogans which were extremely varied, but nevertheless became familiar to the consumer through frequent and long repetition, was typical of the period. A 1910

advertising handbook written by Ernest Spiers stressed the need for both variation and a consistent framework:

> Variety is charming, but a little sameness is also beneficial ... many a firm has made its name by the use of a fantastically shaped name or word constantly repeated, and which becomes known after a time as the firm's sign, similar to a trade mark.[43]

This may suggest the hazy beginnings of an awareness of the importance of closely-defined brand image. However, it is also possible that the multifarious nature of advertising for such products as soap demonstrates an effective approach to a market which was riven with huge social contrasts. Could looser brand images appeal to more varied consumers? Persil washing powder was launched in the United Kingdom in 1907.[44] A series of advertisements in *Home Chat* that year display a variety of graphic approaches – the brand name is written in a different typeface each time, different arrangements of text are used and decorative elements and illustrations are very varied. Yet nevertheless, the advertisements do have a certain consistency – their size never alters and their position on the page is almost always the same. The word Persil, although it looks different each time, is always the largest individual element, and usually appears in the same place within the advertisement. Although the copy varies, several slogans (most prominently 'No boil, no toil') appear over and over again.[45] Were these images crude and undeveloped in terms of brand-management, or did they provide consistency within the framework of variety, as Ernest Spiers, quoted above, suggests?

Some readings – 'frayed garments'

In early 1905 both the upmarket *Queen* magazine and the penny weekly *Home Chat* carried the same advertisement for Sunlight soap (Figure 4.3). A tired housewife scrubs dispiritedly at washing in a tub, enveloped by clouds of steam. Her irritable husband stands in the doorway, and underneath the copy reads: 'Don't let steam and suds be your husband's

4.2 Advertisement for Pears Soap (*The Illustrated London News*, 15 March 1884, p. 263). This advertisement, featuring Mrs Lillie Langtree, shows just one of the many approaches used in Victorian advertising – the use of celebrity endorsements.

DON'T let steam and suds be your husband's welcome on wash-day.

DON'T let tired limbs and frayed garments be the result of your wash.

Sunlight Soap

does away with rubbing and scrubbing, and makes washing easy.

Sunlight Soap is pure, and is made at a model factory in the model village of Port Sunlight.

IT IS NO DEARER THAN COMMON SOAPS.

LEVER BROTHERS, LIMITED, PORT SUNLIGHT, ENGLAND.
The name LEVER on soap is a guarantee of purity and excellence.

4.3 Advertisement for Sunlight soap (*Home Chat*, 4 March 1905, p. 525). This advertisement was also shown in the *Queen* (11 February 1905, unnumbered page). The image's juxtaposition of a housewife who has to do her own washing rather than employing help, and a husband wearing the stiff white collar of the professional, hints at a certain class ambiguity, which may have been intentional on the part of the advertiser.

welcome on wash-day. Don't let tired limbs and frayed garments be the result of your wash.' This final section suggests how some of the issues of class and context raised thus far might be applied to this advertisement.

For the reader of the *Queen*, this advertisement may not have been relevant in offering her, personally, an easier task on washday; primary and secondary sources make it clear that she was likely to have had a laundry maid or maids, the services of a visiting laundress, or to send her washing out to a commercial laundry.[46] Nevertheless, in all but the largest households wash-day was a day of disruption and inconvenience, distracting the servants from the production of meals, and quite possibly filling the house with steam and wet washing.[47] There was also the growing servant problem to be aware of – products which could make the servant's lot easier would have been of increasing interest to any mistress anxious to retain her staff.[48] One of the Persil advertisements already discussed makes an outright claim to be 'another solution to the servant problem'.[49] It is perhaps with these factors in mind that the reader of the *Queen* viewed the Sunlight soap advertisement, though we cannot know whether they persuaded her to buy the product or not.

For the less well-off readers of *Home Chat* who also saw the Sunlight advertisement, washing was equally disruptive (an article in the *Girl's Own Paper* in 1880 on 'washing in a two-up-two-down' describes a day of 'domestic misery and discomfort ... the scolding wife, the truant husband ... neglected children, meals ill-prepared'),[50] but in addition to the inconvenience, the sheer physical toil of washday was a source of dread. According to one of Maud Pember Reeves's informants in her study of slum life in Lambeth, 'you'd expect ter be a bit done-like washin'-day'.[51] Doing the laundry was one of those tasks which could sap the unassisted housewife's strength, undermining the delicate balance between the need for cleanliness and order, and the need for the wife to preserve her health. This balance was crucial to the well-being of the whole family:

> The effective cleanliness of [the] household strikes a subtle balance between more contending needs than can be fully traced out ... If [the housewife] did not sometimes 'let things rip' and take leisure, her health, and with it the whole delicate organisation of the household, would go wrong.[52]

In this instance, laundry becomes an issue of some importance; if Sunlight soap could really make it an easier task, it deserved the attention of the hard-pressed housewife, though again we have no way of knowing if the advertisement actually managed to induce women to buy the product.

We should also consider the attitude which the social classes took to each other's standards of washing and cleanliness – this was an activity in which class prejudices ran rife; would such preconceptions, deployed in an active effort at self-definition within the class system, have affected the way readers of the *Queen* or *Home Chat* looked at the Sunlight image? Mrs Bosanquet, writing in 1896 on divisions within the working classes, observed that 'the luxuries of the lower class become the necessities of the higher', with one of those necessities being cleanliness.[53] Cleanliness, expressed in the very potent symbol of clean white washing, becomes a marker of status. From the middle-class point of view, in 1904 a professional witness cited in the Report of the Inter-Departmental Committee on Physical Deterioration contended that many working-class housewives were 'tainted with incurable laziness and distaste for the obligations of domestic life'.[54] Here again we can imagine a soap advertisement as a focal point for the middle class's perceived superiority over the 'great unwashed'.

Conclusion: frayed meanings

The Sunlight advertisement, with its graphic depiction of the misery and toil of washday, the gendered nature of the task, and the suggestion that a consumer product can ease the burden of domestic drudgery, and improve its results, says much about domesticity, laundry and home life in 1905. It can suggest very forcefully the messages which advertisers thought were effective, messages which increasingly came to shape consumer opinion (though to exactly what extent and in what ways is a point of enormous conjecture). But we should look at advertisements as historical evidence with due caution and consideration. They found their way into a web of media which meant that they were viewed by varied and complicated audiences. Given this, the sort of interpretation of advertisements which slices them from the pages of magazines and subjects each individual image to a virtuoso and isolated semiotic interpretation may miss some of the points which a more complicated, holistic and contextualised approach may catch. Perhaps coming up with a single reading for historical advertising images is not enough – we should consider the possibility of each image being read in different ways by different groups of viewers, and, therefore, be prepared to offer alternative readings ourselves. We should also do what we can to check the readings we propose against sources other than the advertisement itself. Sunlight soap claimed to prevent frayed garments; the historian, on the other hand, should actively pursue 'frayed' meanings, seeking to create historical interpretations that variously reflect the tangled threads of real life.

Notes

1 G.W.Goodall, *Advertising: A Study of a Modern Business Power* (London: Constable, 1914), pp.74–75.

2 Jonathan Rose, *The Intellectual Life of the British Working Classes* (New Haven and London: Yale University Press, 2001), p.4.

3 The ongoing project from which this paper stems is a PhD study which aims to uncover attitudes towards cleanliness in the late nineteenth and early twentieth centuries.

4 Lady Florence Bell, *At the Works: A Study of a Manufacturing Town* (London: Edward Arnold, 1907), chapter vii.

5 Rose, *Intellectual Life*, p.1, gives examples of historians who think the task impossible. Practitioners of cultural studies have been more optimistic, especially for more recent periods. Alison Clarke's study of Tupperware in America, which uses anthropological techniques and oral history, is a good example of a study which uncovers the voice of the historical consumer. Alison J.Clarke, *Tupperware: The Promise of Plastic in 1950s America* (Washington and London: Smithsonian Institute Press, 1999).

6 'He' is used deliberately. The staff of advertising agencies at this time were usually, but not exclusively, men. Nevett notes that male staff members were replaced by women, on a temporary basis, during the First World War (T.R.Nevett, *Advertising in Britain*, London: Heinemann, 1982). However it seems safe, in the pre-1914 period, to refer to the advertising agent as 'he'.

7 Although some of these books do not concern themselves with advertising. In contrast, Ellen Gruber Garvey and Jennifer Scanlon both dealing with American periodicals, address head-on the relationship between editors and journalists, advertisers, and readers on the pages of women's magazines. E.Gruber Garvey, *The Adman in the Parlor* (New York: Oxford University Press, 1996); J.Scanlon, *Inarticulate Longings – The Ladies' Home Journal, Gender, and the Promises of Consumer Culture* (New York and London: Routledge, 1995).

8 R.Ballaster, M.Beetham, E.Frazer and S.Hebron (eds), *Women's Worlds: Ideology, Femininity and the Woman's Magazine* (London: Macmillan, 1991); Margaret Beetham, *A Magazine of Her Own: Domesticity and Desire in the Woman's Magazine, 1800–1914* (London: Routledge, 1996).

9 Ballaster *et al.*, *Women's Worlds*, pp.96–97.

10 Ballaster *et al.*, *Women's Worlds*, p.80; David Reed, *The Popular Magazine in Britain and the United States, 1880–1960* (London: The British Library, 1997), p.80.

11 See, for instance, Richard D.Altick, *The English Common Reader: A Social*

History of the Mass Reading Public 1800–1900 (Columbus: Ohio State University Press, 2nd edn, 1998, first published 1957), p. 380.

12 Margaret Beetham and Kay Boardman (eds), *Victorian Women's Magazines: An Anthology* (Manchester: Manchester University Press, 2001), p. 87.

13 To the extent that *Reynolds's* and *Lloyds'* have been studied by historians, it is their earlier days as Chartist mouthpieces in the mid-nineteenth century which has received attention. Virginia Berridge, 'Popular Sunday Papers and Mid-Victorian Society', in George Boyce, James Curran and Pauline Wingate (eds), *Newspaper History from the Seventeenth Century to the Present Day* (London: Constable, 1978), pp. 246–264.

14 Garvey, *The Adman in the Parlor*, p. 11.

15 See Ellen Mazur Thomson, *The Origins of Graphic Design in America 1870–1920* (New Haven and London: Yale University Press, 1997), chapter 1, for a good round-up of developing reprographic techniques at this period.

16 Beetham and Boardman, *Victorian Women's Magazines*, p. 157.

17 Although we should of course be aware that at this period 'working class' covers everyone from the extremely poor, whose purchasing decisions were very limited, right up to the relative comfort of the skilled trades, whose practitioners could earn as much as the clerks and small shopkeepers who struggled at the lower end of the middle class.

18 Nevett, *Advertising in Britain*, pp. 99–109.

19 Goodall, 1914, p. 58. See p. 19 for an early example of the use of the term 'campaign' in an advertising context. At this date the term 'publicity' is used, but 'marketing' has not yet emerged in its modern sense.

20 Examples include Mather & Crowther's *Practical Advertising: A Handy Guide for Practical Men*, published every year or two years from the 1890s onwards, and Smith's Advertising Agency's *Successful Advertising: its Secrets Explained*, which ran from the 1880s.

21 Richards, *Commodity Culture*, pp. 10–13.

22 Goodall, *Advertising*, p. 20.

23 Mather & Crowther, *Practical Advertising*, p. xxvi.

24 See, for instance, Lynda Nead, *Victorian Babylon: People, Streets and Images in Nineteenth-century London* (New Haven and London: Yale University Press, 2000); Erika Diane Rappaport, *Shopping for Pleasure: Women in the Making of London's West-end* (Princeton and Oxford: Princeton University Press, 2000); Judith Walkowitz, *City of Dreadful Delight: Narratives of Sexual Danger in Late-Victorian London* (Chicago: University of Chicago Press, 1992).

25 Clarence Moran, *The Business of Advertising* (London: Methuen, 1905), pp. 64–65.

26 Goodall, *Advertising*, p. 26.

27 Samuel Deacon & Co. advertising agency, *Deacon's Newspaper Handbook and Advertiser's Guide* (London: Samuel Deacon, 1893), pp. 37–38.

28 Charles Wilson, *The History of Unilever: A Study in Economic Growth and Social Change* (London: Cassell, 1970, first published 1954), vol. I, p. 53. See also Lever Brothers' house magazine, *Progress*, in the 1900s and 1910s, for photographs of decorated vans used in such processions.

29 *Myra's Journal*, 1 April 1895, p. iv.

30 The *Queen*, 19 October 1895, unnumbered advertising page; *Reynolds's Newspaper*, 27 August 1905, p. 7. The *Queen* advertisement is a composite which also contains the image of a mother holding a baby, and copy relating to it. This image and very similar copy was used in *Reynolds's Newspaper* on 12 March 1899, p. 5.

31 Christopher Breward has discussed the readership of *Myra's*, noting that it may have been very diverse, encompassing servants as well as their mistresses, and working-class women in the fashion trades. Christopher Breward, 'Femininity and Consumption: The Problem of the Late Nineteenth-century Fashion Journal', *Journal of Design History*, 7:2 (1994), 72–74.

32 Beetham, *A Magazine of Her Own*, pp. 89–90.

33 Beetham, *Ibid.*, p. 98.

34 Lady Bell, *At the Works*, p. 145.

35 Ernest A. Spiers, *The Art of Publicity* (London: T. Fisher Unwin, 1910), p. 47; Goodall, *Advertising*, p. 32.

36 Mather & Crowther, *Practical Advertising*, p. xlii.

37 Richards, *Commodity Culture*, p. 8.

38 Spiers, *The Art of Publicity*, p. 35; Mather & Crowther, *Practical Advertising*, p. xxviii.

39 Mather & Crowther, *Practical Advertising*, p. lx; see also Spiers, *The Art of Publicity*, p. 56; Moran, *The Business of Advertising*, pp. 15–16.

40 Mather & Crowther, *Practical Advertising*, p. xxii; Moran, *The Business of Advertising*, pp. 6–7.

41 Mike Dempsey, *Bubbles: Early Advertising Art from A. & F. Pears Ltd* (London: Fontana, 1978), examples throughout.

42 Dempsey, *Bubbles*, p. 4; the *Queen*, 20 March 1915, p. 4.

43 Spiers, *The Art of Publicity*, p. 4.

44 A. E. Musson, *Enterprise in Soap and Chemicals: Crosfield's of Warrington 1815–1965* (Manchester: Manchester University Press, 1965), p. 200.

45 *Home Chat*, 2 Jan. 1909, p. ii; 9 Jan., p. ii; 16 Jan., p. ii; 23 Jan., p. ii; 30 Jan.,

p. ii; 13 Feb., p. ii; 20 Feb., p. 469; 27 Feb., p. ii.

46 Christina Hardyment, *From Mangle to Microwave: The Mechanisation of Household Work* (Cambridge: Polity Press, 1988), p. 60; Christina Walkley and Vanda Foster, *Crinolines and Crimping Irons: Victorian Clothes: How They were Cleaned and Cared for* (London: Peter Owen, 1978), p. 54.

47 Walkley and Foster, *Crinolines and Crimping Irons*, p. 54.

48 Hardyment, *Mangle to Microwave*, pp. 61–63.

49 *Home Chat*, 23 January 1909, p. ii.

50 Walkley and Foster, *Crinolines and Crimping Irons*, p. 56.

51 Maud Pember Reeves, *Round About a Pound a Week* (London: G. Bell, 1913), p. 159. See also Lady Bell, *At the Works*, p. 231.

52 Stephen Reynolds, *A Poor Man's House* (London: John Lane, 1909), p. 94.

53 Mrs Bernard (Helen) Bosanquet, *Rich and Poor* (London: Macmillan, 1896), pp. 97–98.

54 *Report of the Inter-Departmental Committee on Physical Deterioration* (London: HMSO, 1904), p. 40.

5 ✦ Domesticating modernity:
Woman magazine and the modern home

Trevor Keeble

I N JULY 1952 the Council of Industrial Design (CoID) appointed
Mary Grieve, editor of *Woman*, to its membership.[1] Seen as a possible
attempt to counter accusations of middle-class bias, it is assumed
that Grieve's election to the principal institution of post-war taste-making
must have exposed her readership to something of its influence; and that
this factor undoubtedly figured large in the Council's decision to invite
her to join.[2] This essay attempts to analyse and explain some of the issues
regarding the attitudes, tone and terminology of material presented by
the Home editorial pages of *Woman* magazine during this period.

The CoID's decision to co-opt *Woman* magazine represents something of a departure for the organisation. Previously, the CoID attempted
to communicate its agenda and reform ideals through very specific
design-focused events and publications, such as the 'Britain Can Make
It' exhibition of 1946, the Festival of Britain in 1951, the publication of
Design magazine from 1949, and the collaboration with Penguin Books
on a series of designed oriented thematic studies entitled *The Things We
See* (1947). This change of approach articulates the extent to which it
was recognised that the quite dogmatic rhetoric employed by this government body needed to be rationalised, explained and ultimately mediated
by a mass-readership publication.

Using the magazine as a case study this essay discusses popular
representations of domestic modernity in the 1950s. It also draws upon
the critical ideas of Pierre Bourdieu and the British sociologist of post-war
domestic spaces, Dennis Chapman. Their work is employed as a means
of identifying and interpreting the content of the magazine, and allows

a more nuanced and developed discussion of the role of the magazine in the transmission of domestic design advice. The essay highlights the significant position that the magazine held by conditioning and verifying the tastes and desires of mass readerships. This work proposes that it is within the ephemeral and responsive arena of periodical publishing that we might find a more sophisticated and realistic mirror of popular attitudes to issues such as domestic modernity than was available through the 'professional' arena of design and design reform.

Addressing the reader

The publication of *Woman* magazine in 1937 was significant because of its emphasis on colour. Published and printed by Odhams at their Watford plant, the magazine introduced the visual stimulation of the photogravure printing technique to the women's weekly magazine market.[3] After an initially disappointing two years, Mary Grieve was appointed editor of the magazine in 1939 – a position she held until 1964.[4] Perhaps the most celebrated of women editors, Mary Grieve's tenure at *Woman* witnessed a strategic reformulation of the role of the modern women's magazine and its position within its readers' life. At the centre of this strategy was a policy of 'reader identification', which was used to reinforce the links between magazine and reader, and ensure that the editorial content of the publication engaged and reflected the lives of its readership.[5] Cynthia White has noted the significance of the readers' letter page in this development and has suggested that it 'opened up a channel of communication through which women could exchange the fascinating trivia of everyday life.'[6] Selling at a cover price of 4½d (equivalent to about 2p) throughout the early 1950s, *Woman* magazine, along with *Woman's Illustrated* (1936) and *Woman's Own* (1932) has been credited as being among the first of the middle-class weeklies to become a mass circulation periodical.[7] Although originally aimed toward a middle-class market, the aspirational nature of magazine reading during this period, and *Woman* magazine's unparalleled successful expansion, meant that by the 1950s it sold over 2 million copies per issue.[8] The subsequent handing-on of each issue between readers undoubtedly meant that the magazine reached a cross-section of women, many of whom were working class.

The beginning of the 1950s was marked by an increased specialisation in the areas covered by *Woman* magazine. Editorial departments evolved to address what were considered to be the many facets of a woman's life. At the head of each department was an editor whose name became synonymous with the subject of that department. During the period under study, all advice about clothing and fashion was given by the fashion editor, Veronica Scott; all personal advice offered through 'Evelyn Home's Problem Page'; and all lessons in the art of cookery given by Ruth Morgan in her column entitled 'Ruth Morgan's Cookery Course', which later became 'The Wooden Spoon Club'. The personal nature of this approach meant that the reader could effectively build a relationship with the experts, and thus a feeling of trust in the magazine was gained. Once established, the format for each editorial department rarely changed. The one exception to this 'unwritten' rule was the home department presided over by Edith Blair.

The diversity of subjects covered by the home department such as cleaning, mending, decorating, furnishing and entertaining in the home required a variety of different approaches, all of which maintained an advisory nature.[9] It was on this area of home design advice that the Council of Industrial Design sought to bear its influence. The CoID was established in Britain under the auspices of the Board of Trade in 1944. The organisation developed the agenda of the Utility scheme, which was implemented in 1941 to ensure provision of clothing and domestic furnishing during the war.[10] Although ostensibly intended to emphasise the role of design within industry, the Council also sought to heighten the awareness of design issues, and reform the taste of the consuming public.[11] In this sense, it actively sought to engage popular opinion and educate it in the appreciation of 'good design'. This model of good design advice clearly asserts a modernist agenda of rationalisation, efficiency and explicit 'modernity' in regard to domestic design.[12]

All design advice occupies a specific temporal position, deriving from accumulated knowledge and custom. As a model, it is a conception of its creators, designed to address a necessarily different conception held by its intended receiver or subject. As such, design advice constitutes a tangible attempt to alter the disposition of its intended receiver. The professional design establishment's concerns about the standards of public taste range across society and boundaries of class. Thus, the need to impart the ideals of the highbrow design professional goes beyond the gender division which it created to address the changing character of the working classes during this period, which, I would argue, by virtue of the divisions of responsibility, were markedly feminine in their aesthetic and material conditions.

In her essay 'Making Yourself at Home: A Study in Discourse', Valerie Swales attempts to characterise a subjectivity based upon 'common sense values'. She suggests that,

> All individuals act through and upon common sense values, which are both kept in place, but also continually transformed, by actions, thoughts and intersubjective experience. Common sense knowledge can be said to be both structured and structuring in its action and is always open to restatement in accordance with new situations.[13]

Swales's thesis, which draws largely on Pierre Bourdieu's concept of 'habitus', makes clear the degree to which 'common sense knowledge' is in itself evolutionary and as such, subject to external influence. The concept of 'habitus' was developed by Bourdieu as a tool for investigating the social practice of individuals in their everyday lives.[14] In essence the habitus constitutes the dispositions and classificatory schemes of individuals' taste within the context of their society and environment, as explained by Daniel Miller,

> The concept of perspective implies that understanding is derived from a particular position in the world. If two groups have different perspectives, then in so far as they are able to create the world, they naturally do so in accordance with their own perspective.[15]

Put simply, the habitus informs the ordering of objects in an environment in a way that constitutes 'taste'. This complex and, at times, highly theoretical concept is used by Bourdieu as part of a much wider equation which seeks to examine social practice. Within this wider concept, habitus is viewed as having a direct relationship with 'capital', which as the term suggests, carries connotations of cultivation and production. It is important to state that 'habitus' and 'capital' are mutually dependent, and neither is offered dominance over the other. The concept of capital is differentiated and is used in Bourdieu's sense as 'economic capital', 'social capital', 'cultural capital' and 'symbolic capital'. It is the latter categories, those of 'cultural' and 'symbolic' capital, which are most useful to this study of taste-making and are worthy of further explanation.

Cultural capital has been identified as 'primarily legitimate knowledge of one kind or another'.[16] This can be viewed more generally, as largely conscious knowledge, something that is, in some way tangible and can be articulated or taught. Education is the most explicit form for the cultivation of cultural capital, although the development of cultural capital is by no means confined to the formal practices of education. Symbolic capital has been typified as 'prestige' or 'honour'.[17] This, in contrast to cultural capital, is often largely unconscious in all but effect, and as such is less tangible and more socially constructed. Symbolic capital, as a result, is more apparent in an identified social group or class, to both members 'within' this group and those 'outside' it. Much of the information presented within *Woman* magazine might be analysed in the terms of cultural or symbolic capital, and the magazine as a whole can be used to illustrate the extent to which 'information' or 'advice' negotiates and attempts to revise established or traditional knowledge and patterns of life.

Arising from a masculine and public field of 'production', the agenda of design reform during the 1950s, was derived from a very different 'logic' to that held by its intended subject, the working-class female homemaker. The 'capital' informing each of these two fields is as diverse as the habitus which governs its actions. This does not mean that cultural and symbolic capital does not hold currency in its transference from one field to another, but that if it does, it is because it 'shares' in some way, consciously or unconsciously a 'code', it has something common to both fields of activity. The CoIDs attempt to access the pages of *Woman* magazine during the early 1950s represents a very specific attempt to bridge the rhetorical gap between the professional sphere of design production and the realm of domestic consumption.

The analysis of the home and its inhabitation was the subject of increasing sociological study during this period. One such study entitled *The Home and Social Status* by Dennis Chapman, published in 1955, has provided great insight into the accepted views and opinions surrounding the domestic sphere and its various meanings during the 1950s.[18] Drawing upon the influential work of the mass observation studies conducted since 1937, Dennis Chapman's work attempts to engage and explore the use of sociological theory within the realm of observation study and as such it is a formative example of the modern sociological attempt to explicitly rationalise both 'qualitative' and 'quantitative' research and evidence.[19] With its emphasis upon the relationship between the lived experience of particular domestic conditions and the wider connotations of status and class identity, Chapman's work anticipates many of the broad themes developed by Bourdieu in his study *Distinction: A Social Critique of the Judgement of Taste*.[20] Chapman's study highlights an accepted differentiation and hierarchy of spaces, and his introduction in the form of a 'Method and Basic Hypothesis' provides a concise summary of factors worth bearing in mind whilst considering much of the design advice detailed in *Woman* magazine.

> Much of the discussion will be about the change in domestic functions and the relation between 'manifest functions', which are intended and consciously acknowledged, and those 'latent functions' which arise from a variety of forces which may not be intended or acknowledged by the participants. It is characteristic that latent functions as they emerge become consciously and intentionally pursued and join the complex of 'manifest functions'. This complex of manifest functions, latent functions and corresponding disfunctions of the family and its members presents the performance requirements of the home. The conflicts between these and the mechanical abstractions of the sanitary engineer, architect and designer are an important social problem.[21]

Chapman's categorisation of 'manifest' and 'latent' functions provide a useful model with which to examine the information published by *Woman*, and it is worth comparing the broad characteristics of these 'functions' to the models used by Bourdieu, outlined earlier. Like 'cultural' capital, the 'manifest' function is identified as 'intended and consciously acknowledged'. Conversely, the 'latent' function is identified as possibly not 'intended or acknowledged', a characteristic shared by Bourdieu's 'symbolic' capital. This correlation, though crude, expresses and articulates the essential differences between the interests of the homemaker and those of the design professional. The position of the magazine in the changing culture of the 1950s was noted by Chapman as central to the phenomenon of 'conscious social differentiation' and constituted part of the 'widespread complex social, educational, "cultural" and economic

movement'[22] of the period. Not surprisingly, given the critical focus
upon the nature of social status, Chapman's work implicates women's
magazines within a broader daily and architectural press, which finds
reinforcement of its agenda from 'the state' through the authority of its
Council of Industrial Design. This agenda is identified as being one of
'education and propaganda'.[23]

Woman visits the new homemakers

In its bid to identify with the reader, the Home Department of *Woman*
developed a number of quite strategic approaches to exemplify good
domestic design. During the early years of the 1950s these took the
form of series and articles concerning identified people and their own
domestic arrangements. Using such a method, the Home Department
showed by example the implications of domestic design on patterns of
living. Though published irregularly throughout the period, these articles
supplement the more general advice about the beautification and reno-
vation of the home and largely form the basis of the following analysis
of how the home was represented in its entirety.

For example, the first edition of *Woman* in 1952 ran an article entitled 'Showhouse Becomes A Home'. The showhouse in Peterlee, a 'new
town' in the north-east of England, was noted as having been furnished
and decorated by the Council of Industrial Design. The construction
and display of public showhouses by the CoID had begun as part of
the activities of the 'Festival of Britain' and the results were found to be
favourable: 'This work was agreed to be a useful activity, since the influence of the houses on residents in the new towns could be considerable
and yet the cost to the council and committee was small.'[24] The project at
Peterlee had actually built two showhouses, one of which was decorated
entirely in the 'contemporary' style and the other combining 'old' and
'new'. Both houses were opened for view by the Secretary of the National
Union of Mineworkers on 26 July 1951. At the 59th meeting of the CoID,
it was noted that,

> In spite of the rather isolated position of the houses attendance at both
> the opening of the houses and during the five weeks' showing was
> very good and the houses had to be kept open for longer hours than
> originally intended. Miss Pirie's practical schemes were colourful and

attractive, and the corporation was delighted with the results ... The success of the showhouses at Hatfield and Peterlee as an economical way of introducing well designed goods to new areas and of persuading retailers to stock contemporary furniture has encouraged us to approach other new towns and local authorities where local rebuilding is being carried out.[25]

Describing the house for the readers of *Woman*, Edith Blair writes,

> Here in ordinary small rooms, the designers' use gaily patterned wallpapers in new ways, show new combinations of colour, and show us how the sturdy, clean limbed furniture will mix with the old. This is a problem that faces us all. But however exciting it is to look at an exhibition house and gather new ideas from it, a house is built to be lived in. New kinds of flooring, different arrangements of rooms, gay colour combinations, a new fuel-saving fire, all may have gone through rigorous experimental tests but it's the test of everyday living that really counts.[26]

At the close of the exhibition, we are informed that John and Betty Surtees and their six-year-old son Tony became the first tenants of the new home. John, twenty-eight, had been a miner for fourteen years and for seven years he and Betty had shared the homes of relatives where, the reader is told, 'They lived in the shadow of the slag heap, in a narrow street where front doors open straight onto the pavement, where the only living things are the plants in front windows and the grass that grows over derelict patches.'[27] This article firmly establishes the social problems faced by young families in the early post-war era, and the conditions of newly-weds living in cramped conditions with in-laws is a theme which the magazine addresses and develops over a number of years. Having described how taken John and Betty were with the new 'one wall' papering scheme, which Edith Blair cites as the answer to the 'small room problem', and a feature that was to become regularly prominent in her 'Tackle it Together' pages, she discusses the layout of rooms. Blair concludes, 'The architects have reversed the order of living round here, where the centre of family life is the kitchen. They've made the kitchen a narrow but efficient, workroom and provided a centrally heated dining room opening out of it for meals.'[28]

The language of the article clearly indicates the need, on the part of John and Betty, to adapt from the 'old' to the 'new' and the reasoning behind this is explained in terms of problems, answers and efficiency. Finally, Edith Blair adds reassuringly that 'Betty was particularly taken with the "utility" room, a new name for the scullery.' Couching the 'new' within the terminology of the old, Edith Blair presents this home as an evolution from the familiar.

Although only a single article in an expanse of 'other' information, Blair's analysis of the Surtees' adaption to their new home presents the reader with a clear vision of an ensuing modernity. The 'Showhouse Becomes a Home' article instigates a mode of domestic representation, which clearly sought to situate domestic design reform within an identifiable social context. Whereas previous attempts by the CoID had created fictional rooms for fictional families, in the pages of *Woman* domestic design was presented as a 'reality'.[29] Through its presentation of a real family in a real home, *Woman* magazine necessarily engaged issues of social status and class but did so within its remit of 'reader identification'. Whilst never alluding to such sociological models as outlined above, it is evident that the editors of the magazine had an innate sensibility concerning how educational information must be couched and presented within a readily identifiable context.

The form of representation and the issues introduced by the 'showhouse' article were to become formalised and clarified in a number of series, which focused upon real homes and real homemakers. The first, and perhaps most significant of these was a six-part series published in 1953 entitled 'Woman Visits the New Homemakers' (see Figures 5.1 and 5.2). This feature claimed, 'we present these homes, some traditional, some experimental, all full of interest to give a fresh outlook on a home of your own'.[30] The series was edited by Edith Blair, who incorporated the assistance of the newly appointed *Woman* Consultant Architect, Patricia J. Owen ARIBA, AA Diploma. No reference is made to Miss Owen's involvement with the Council of Industrial Design or its 1946 publication, *Furnishing to Fit the Family*.[31] Although limited to only six studies of new homemakers, the series focused on newly built properties and their different implications on living. Presented in a similar format, these articles included plans and at times considerable technical information regarding construction. As with the showhouse article, the homemakers were readily identified, even if idealised.

The emphasis for this new series on homes was economy and

innovation. The first article, entitled 'We Built Our House in an Old World Garden', tells the story of Eileen and William Worthy and their two children, Susan and Richard. Whilst explaining the circumstances of obtaining the land, Edith Blair notes that William works in real estate. She proceeds to explain the Worthy's requirements of their architect,

5.1 'Tall town house' from '*Woman* visits the new homemakers' series, *Woman*, 7 November 1953. This article illustrates a contemporary interior comprising lightwood plywood furniture, understated décor and contemporary furnishings. Much is made of the efficient plan of the house, which is clearly shown for all four floors. As with the other articles in the series, these plans convey a very strict ordering of functional spaces the homemakers featured in this article are shown in consultation with their 'bearded' architect.

a kitchen as mechanically perfect as possible to save both time and labour … The kitchen has everything for saving time and labour. A solid fuel cooker and water heater fulfils all duties for about ten shillings a week upkeep and Patricia Owen was particularly happy to see that all available wall space was filled with roomy cupboards.[32]

5.2 'A barn becomes a lovely home' from '*Woman* visits the new homemakers' series, *Woman*, 14 November 1953. This is the only feature in the series that presented a converted building as a home. This feature presents the modernisation of an old vernacular building. However, in doing so, the vernacular characteristics of this building remain prominent. Although modern in its spatial arrangement, this home is presented as distinctly 'old' in character.

Presented in colour photographs of both the interior and the exterior, the house is portrayed as being comprehensively modern. Much is made of the windows, particularly the large living room window, which, we are informed, is 'known in America as a picture window because it frames the view'. Elsewhere, the windows have been used strategically,

> Windows are a big feature of the whole house. The dining room end of the long living room has an east window which means sun – if there is any – for breakfast. French windows lead to the garden and there's another French window, sitting room end.[33]

The possibility of adapting this house to the changing needs of its occupants is raised, as Edith Blair describes how the children's bedroom has been specially designed so that as they grow older it can be partitioned. This consideration is continued downstairs, where in the design process an area had been earmarked for any future developments that might be needed. The only distinct requirement apparent so far was the need for a utility room. At the personal request of William, the architect supplied a large bathroom to accommodate, what Edith Blair describes to be his 'Richard Dimbleby frame' and for Eileen 'a large fireplace for the sitting room'. In awarding this house full marks, Patricia Owen and Edith Blair sum up its achievements, 'Not an inch of waste, and yet it never appears cramped.' (The double-page colour spread also features 'Building Notes' by Patricia Owen; these include comments about the chimney stack not spoiling the effect of the ridge line and details the specification of roof and cavity wall insulation.)

Many of the issues raised by this first article appeared in a second, which was illustrated in the same format, '"House of Adventure" tells the story of a new home and a new neighbourhood both of which are experiments in living'.[34]

After recounting the details of costs, Edith Blair explains how the architect, Fred Pooley, designed the house for himself, his wife and their three children,

> Fred Pooley as deputy architect to the city of Coventry is helping to plan and design the houses and flats for a new housing centre on the fringe of Coventry – and living himself among the factory workers of this new area.

In this new centre of between 6,000 and 7,000 inhabitants, Coventry wants those who work in the factory and those who employ to live alongside each other – not in isolated districts. The village community, up to date.[35]

This utopian vision is realised on much the same lines as the previous property. However, under inspection, aspects of the rhetoric employed go further. Discussing the 'feeling of space inside this house' Edith Blair comments that, 'Wherever you look inside there's a view and a sense of space. The front door opens onto a view through the hall to French windows at the back.' This effect is heightened by the partial separation of the kitchen from the living room by a counter and frame-work. Originally conceived as an attempt at cost cutting, this feature is explained according to the rationalist overtones of modernist design reform discourse. Remarking on Fred's innovation, Blair reiterates that Fred's, 'Answer begins with his downright assertion that a lot of things we live with and consider necessities, could be painlessly parted with – walls for instance!' The absence of walls, as the plans that accompany this article show, is taken to a conclusion upstairs where only the bathroom is actually walled. The rest of the space is described as 'one sleeping area subdivided into cubicles', each with a curtained wall on to a corridor. Perhaps not surprisingly, 'Hilda finds this arrangement works very well. Whereas in their other flats and houses she always left the children's doors open at night, and the sitting-room door, too, now there's no open door inconvenience.'[36]

This quite insistent rationalisation of spatial arrangement naturally extends to the kitchen where, it is indicated, Hilda can set out meals in two smooth operations with no time-wasting. Describing the residents as a naturally tidy and quiet family, Edith Blair makes comparisons between the house and a ship, concluding that like a ship 'it instils is own discipline of living'.

Amongst the explanations of low costs and efficiency, the house does have a single extravagance. Described as 'a sheer luxury' and 'a concession to Hilda', the open fireplace consumes £8 of coal a year, 'not necessary expenditure because the room is perfectly comfortable without a fire in winter'. The engendering of this extravagance as female is part of an ongoing discourse discussed by Dennis Chapman,

The fireplace is one of the most complex socio-technical artefacts of the home. Its primary purpose is space-heating, but it appears to have deep mystical connotation and great aesthetic importance. It locates and focuses the family group in summer and winter. The history of domestic heating appliances for a century or more has been attempts by engineers to produce an efficient space heater, continuously frustrated by the demand of the consumer to have an open fire, the least efficient and dirtiest of all space heating devices. Generally speaking, efficiency plays little part in the design and provision of heating appliances.[37]

The fireplace in the Pooley's home, like that of the Worthy's featured in the previous article, is attributed to be a concession to the woman of the home, thus implicating her directly with the setbacks and frustrations encountered by the engineer. This point is supported by Richard Hoggart who notes that 'the hearth is reserved for the family' and that it subsequently has great importance to the housewife and mother, who 'knows that she must "keep a good fire" and is likely to pay more attention to securing that than to buying the better qualities of warm woollen underclothing: a fire is shared and seen.'[38]

Concluding their article with 'Building Notes' that expound the efficiency of fair faced, sand-lime brickwork and light steel lattice beams, not to mention roofs of corrugated asbestos, Edith Blair and Patricia Owen came away from the 'experimental' house, 'agreeing that owning a home is within the grasp of many more young people if they are prepared to follow the new designs'.[39] Presenting these case studies, Edith Blair offers the reader an insight into 'modern' living, which though disciplined by its new surroundings, finds resounding support in the testimonies of the inhabitants.

What is significant about the '*Woman* Visits the New Homemakers' series is that it establishes a somewhat 'domestic' approach to the information concerning the design, construction and decoration of domestic space. Whilst attempting to explain and develop a discussion regarding new forms of domestic design, the magazine retains a largely informal and, therefore, friendly approach. Any distance which might have been felt between the everyday homemaker and the design professional is effectively removed due to the magazine's mediation. Having stated this, Edith Blair and the magazine in general, were not reticent about championing aspects of modern domesticity which the reader may find less appealing. Explaining the merits of an 'open plan house', *Woman* Consultant Architect Patricia J. Owen goes to some length to rationalise this new mode of living in terms of expenditure by identifying, rather problematically, that fewer walls equates with less money spent. This reasoning is developed by Joan Bailey, for whom, 'the joy of this open plan living is the fact that the whole house is in use instead of shutting off parlour or dining room and then having to warm them up when needed, which was the old way of living'.[40]

In its presentation of these newly-built modern homes, *Woman* magazine construed to illuminate the role of the architect and designer. In the everyday language of its readership, a language which emphasised the moral certainties of 'clean-limbed furniture', 'quiet families' and 'tidy kitchens', it sought to explain and justify the intrusions of modernity whilst all the time praising its benefits. In doing so, it trod a very careful line between maintaining the 'modern' cause, to which its editor had been conscripted, and ensuring not to alienate its readers by presenting anything artificial or unrealistic. The '*Woman* Visits the New Home-makers' series establishes the home as an object of both private and professional concern. However, the authority of the design professional is well reaffirmed due to the fact that the series is edited by the *Woman* Consultant Architect, and each of the new homemakers considered has some professional grounding within the field, as either a 'real estate agent', 'local authority architect', 'lecturer in furniture design' or even just as 'friend of an architect'.

Whilst acknowledging its readers' investment of symbolic capital within the sphere of the home, the magazine chose to present the modernity of these new homes through an implicit statement of the cultural capital of the modern homes' inhabitants. The authority of the homemakers presented effectively validates the modernity of these new ways of living and provides both a model for the reader to aspire to, and a clear indication of just how important design consideration within the home should be. In addition to this, the articles provide a tacit example of the role the home may assume in the construction and consolidation of its inhabitant's social identity.

Conclusion

In an unpublished seminar paper entitled 'Families, Their Needs and Preferences in the Home' written in 1949, Dennis Chapman addressed the attempted reform of working-class ideals with regard to domestic space. After a lengthy account of his initial findings concerning the domestic practices of the people of Liverpool, where he taught at the university, he dismissed the CoID's attempts to access a broader audience as having 'aimed too high'.[41] He concluded, 'Perhaps it would be best to approach these families through the sort of publications that they regularly read, the inexpensive women's magazines.'[42]

The changing relationship between the designer and consumer has been identified as central to the conflict within domestic modernity.[43] The proposed divergence of the arenas of domestic design production and consumption suggests, as Dennis Chapman identified in 1949, the need for some mediating forum through which the languages of both production and consumption might be presented in such a manner as to be meaningful. The domestic home advice offered by *Woman* magazine during the first half of the 1950s constitutes such a mediating forum. Having been largely excluded from the paternal authorities of design production, femininity formed in the guise of women's magazines its own 'selective interpretation' of modernity. This interpretation naturally found its basis in domesticity and consumption, the activities of everyday life.

Whilst the critical mechanisms developed by Pierre Bourdieu and Dennis Chapman are necessarily abstract, they allow for a critical interrogation and analysis of the manner in which the producers of *Woman* magazine sought to bridge the increasing divide between the dogmatic agenda of the professional design authorities and the needs and desires of the consuming female householder. This in turn, exposes the importance and ubiquity of the periodical magazine in the transmission of information, knowledge and taste. In the 1950s Mary Grieve's *Woman* magazine articulated a set of values and ideas to a previously unreachable audience. Whether those readers acted upon such advice is another question.

Notes

1 Minutes of the 64th meeting of the Council of Industrial Design at 2.30 p.m. on 11 July 1952. CoID Archive, University of Brighton.

2 J. Woodham, 'Managing British Design Reform I', in the *Journal of Design History*, vol. 9, no. 1, p. 56.

3 C. White, *Women's Magazines 1693–1968* (London; Michael Joseph, 1970) p. 97.

4 J. Winship, *Inside Women's Magazines* (London: Pandora, 1987), p. 20.

5 White, *Women's Magazines*, p. 128. See also, M. Grieve, *Millions Made My Story* (London: Gollancz, 1964).

6 White, *Women's Magazines*, p. 128.

7 Ibid., p. 96.

8 Ibid., Appendix IV, 'Circulation of Principal Women's Weekly "Magazines" 1938–1968'.

9 Whilst the magazine, unlike many of its weekly contemporaries, always engaged the reader's role within the home and the centrality of the domestic sphere within women's lives, the emphasis upon this theme increased during the war years and the subsequent period of austerity which followed. Ibid., chapter 4, 'Utility Journals: 1946–1956', pp. 123–154.

10 See H. Dover, *Home Front Furniture: British Utility Design 1941–1951*. (Aldershot: Scholar Press, 1991); *Utility Furniture and Fashion 1941–1951* (London: The Geffrye Museum, 1995).

11 For a broad discussion of the CoID and its activities see P. Sparke (ed.), *Did Britain Make It? British Design in Context 1946–86* (London: The Design Council, 1986); Woodham, 'Managing British Design Reform I'.

12 A good discussion of the failures of the CoID's attempts to access a popular audience is articulated in S. Macdonald and J. Porter, *Putting on the Style: Setting up Home in the 1950s* (London: The Geffrye Museum, 1990).

13 V. Swales, 'Making Yourself at Home: A Study in Discourse', in T. Putnam and C. Newton (eds), *Household Choices* (London: Future Publications, 1990), p. 103. This is a proposition also used by Scott Oram in his study of popular homemaking during the 1950s: '"Common Sense Contemporary": the ideals and realities of the popular domestic interior of the 1950s' unpublished V&A/RCA MA History of Design dissertation (London: Royal College of Art, 1994). See also Christine Morley's study 'Homemakers and Design Advice in the postwar period', in Putnam and Newton (eds), *Household Choices*.

14 Bourdieu, P. *Distinction: A Social Critique of the Judgement of Taste* (London: Routledge & Kegan Paul, 1984).

15 D. Miller, *Material Culture and Mass Consumption* (Oxford: Basil Blackwell Ltd, 1987) p. 163.

16 R. Jenkins, *Pierre Bourdieu* (London: Routledge, 1992), p. 85.

17 Ibid., p. 85.

18 D. Chapman, *The Home and Social Status* (London: Routledge & Kegan Paul Ltd, 1955), p. vi (republished in 1998 as part of 'The International Library of Sociology' series by Routledge).

19 See B. Highmore, 'Mass Observation: A Science of Everyday Life', in *Everyday Life and Cultural Theory: An Introduction* (London: Routledge, 2002), pp. 75–112.

20 P. Bourdieu, *Distinction: A Social Critique of the Judgement of Taste* (London: Routledge & Kegan Paul Ltd, 1984).

21 Chapman, *The Home and Social Status*, p. 28.

22 Ibid., p. 20.

23 Ibid., p. 21.

24 Minutes of the 58th Meeting of the Council of Industrial Design held on 13 July 1951, CoID Archive.

25 Minutes of the 59th Meeting of the Council of Industrial Design held on 14 September 1951, CoID Archive.

26 *Woman*, W/E 5/1/1952 p. 22.

27 Ibid.

28 Ibid.

29 At the 'Britain Can Make It' exhibition of 1946 the organisers constructed rooms for fictitious families and individuals. These were broadly felt to reflect a highly idealised notion rather than the reality. See P. J. Owen, *Furnishing To Fit The Family* (London: The Council of Industrial Design, 1946).

30 *Woman*, W/E 10 October 1953, p. 22–23.

31 Patricia Jane Owen was registered as a member of the Royal Institute of British Architects from 1936.

32 *Woman*, W/E 10 October 1953 p. 22–23.

33 Ibid.

34 *Woman*, W/E 17 October 1953 p. 24–25.

35 Ibid.

36 Ibid.

37 Chapman, *The Home and Social Status*, p. 96.

38 R. Hoggart, *The Uses of Literacy* (London: Penguin, 1992), p. 35. Originally published London: Chatto & Windus, 1957.

39 *Woman*, W/E 17 October 1953, p. 25.

40 *Woman*, W/E 31 October 1953, p. 22.

41 D. Chapman, 'Families, Their Needs and Preferences in the Home'. Unpublished paper read by Miss Rosemary Frost at an uncited conference on Tuesday 19 July 1955, p. 34. I am most grateful to Christine Morley for providing me with a copy of this typed script which has been annotated by hand 'In the presence of G. Russell'.

42 Ibid.

43 T. Putnam, 'Between Taste and Tradition: Decorative Order in the Modern Home', in *Bulletin of the John Rylands University Library of Manchester*, vol. 77, no. 1, Spring 1995, p. 96.

6 ✧ Black Panthers in *Vogue*: signifying 'blackness' in fashion magazines [1]

Zoé Nicole Whitley

(*To Donna Aurelia Richardson, my mother*)

These are no civil rights Negroes wearing grey suits three sizes too big ... these are real men!

Shoot-outs, revolutions, pictures in Life magazine of policemen grabbing Black Panthers like they were Vietcong – somehow it all runs together in the head with the whole thing of how beautiful they are ... they are so lean, so lithe, as they say, with tight pants and Yoruba-style headdresses, almost like turbans, as if they'd stepped out of the pages of Vogue, although no doubt Vogue got it from them. [2]

I T WAS during the Civil Rights Movement of the 1960s in the United States that a certain sociocultural inscription of black people began to shift fundamentally. The change made itself manifest on American television sets, the front pages of newspapers and poured through visual media the world over. In 1966, the year following the assassination of Malcolm X, Huey P. Newton and Bobby Seale founded the Black Panther Party for Self Defence in Oakland, California; Stokeley Carmichael was credited with conceiving the term 'Black Power' and *Vogue* allowed its first black model, Donyale Luna, to appear on the UK cover of the 1 March edition.

It may seem a bizarre or even arbitrary coupling to pair American race politics with the editorial policies of *Vogue*'s European editions but the two became inextricably linked in the late 1960s. The following exploration focuses on British and Paris *Vogue* situated primarily within the context of twentieth-century American history. This approach accentuates in part the growing influence of American popular culture in Europe, in part the international scope of fashion photography and fashion magazines, and in large part the fact that black America's quest for racial equality – its methods shifting rapidly from passive resistance to the threat of aggression – garnered worldwide if ultimately short-lived interest. This in turn heavily influenced the shaping of what came to be understood as 'black' during the period.

The fundamental tenets of the Black Panther organisation centred on elevating the black community through grass-roots projects such as feeding breakfast to hungry inner-city school children as well as leading the impending violent revolution to dislodge whites from power. The Panthers capitalised on a threatening mystique through carefully assembled physical presentation, often consisting of black leather, turtlenecks, dark sunglasses and Afros. From the outset of their political activism, fashion proved to be a particularly highly contested domain for black women:

> The bourgeois female, young, whorish, working, extremely well dressed … as near in simulated looks and make-up, stance, and blandness as possible to the Glamour-Mademoiselle-Vogue image … uses (and emasculates) her man as a social coat-hanger, a bill payer, a dude, a vehicle to further her own confused self-image.[3]

In this context, what at first seems a trivial connection made between cultural consciousness and dress sense becomes a potent political symbol.

> Elements of 'traditional' African dress – tunics and dashikis, head-wraps and skullcaps, elaborate beads and embroidery – all suggested that black people were contracting out of Westernness and identifying with all things African as a positive alternative … we might also remember that as they filtered through mass media, such as magazines, music or television, these styles contributed to the increasing visibility of black struggles in the 1960s. As elements of everyday life, these black styles in hair and dress helped to underline massive shifts in popular aspirations among black people and participated in a populist logic of rupture.[4]

What happened by the late 1960s was particularly unexpected. Mercer's 'populist logic of rupture' was rapidly defused as a result of sub-cultural commodification by the mainstream culture. As a result of this further shift, far from alienating the white community, Panther chic became alluring. 'The Afro hairstyle in particular became a highly visible yet culturally empty signifier of blackness though it first represented a "reconstitutive link with Africa".[5] A (Black Muslim) article appeared that invalidated the Afro as a sign of racial pride. It declared 'Whites Buying "African Hair" Wigs as "Natural" Hair Style Gains Popularity.' The natural was no longer black.[6]

Many black Americans began acknowledging their African ancestry through a variety of means, adopting for example Afro-American as a defining term while rejecting the epithets Negro and 'colored' which had been imposed upon them and had come to represent the stringent practices of segregation and institutionalised racism.

Many signs and messages are transmitted through an emphasis placed on the surface and the visual. So much was this the case with regard to the aesthetic ushered in by the Black Panther movement that an engagement with the African diaspora – both as a real and an imagined community[7] – was to permeate visual culture on many levels. Not least of these was fashion photography.

Clive Arrowsmith's fashion spread *Afrodizzyaction* appeared in British *Vogue* in September 1969 and demonstrates the excited mainstream imitation the Black Panthers generated. A woman on all fours wears 'African earrings', 'multicoloured and intricate Nigerian bead necklace and belt' and a 'black cire catsuit'. Her impressive Afro is divided into a section of braids in the crown, accented with a fringe of white beads. The Afro is merely one of a selection of 'great wigs by Leonard'. The model is white. On the page opposite the model in the catsuit, another white model is poised as if to pounce, on all fours. She wears a long-sleeve print button-front shirt with a wide collar. She is barefoot and wears a raffia skirt. Her Afro is more impressive than her counterpart's, dark and massive, extending well beyond her shoulders. On the pages that follow are other white models in Afro wigs of varying shades and textures, wearing Dashikis, gold chokers and large gold earrings.

Why the many 'ethnic' details? *Vogue* announces that 'Africa must be the next source of inspirational magic in Fashion land – vibrant colours, brilliant beadwork, mixed-up prints and brave barbaric adornments.' British *Vogue* is relying upon a condensed vision of the continent first used by many black American nationalists in the 1960s. Any attempt at uncovering an authentic aspect of ethnicity has been constructed from a variety of disparate objects assembled to form what is understood as blackness. Of paramount significance is that the inspirational 'Africa' has been imaged without recourse to black people, black skin being the most tangible aspect of racialised identity. Abstracted notions of 'blackness' and the 'exotic' had entered the visual vocabulary of fashion photography.

The wearing of the beads and wigs on the white Arrowsmith models becomes nothing more than a type of offensive mime. The code created by hairstyles, jewellery, textiles and postures to read as 'black' relies especially on two key aspects: the animal and the sexual, notions of the 'exotic' and the 'erotic', respectively.

Recent work on race, pathology and sexuality isolates the human need to create categories, to define others in opposition to the self in order to make sense of the world. Much of this categorisation takes place through identifying differences in physiognomy like skin colour, size and shape of facial features, even differences in genitalia.[8] Sander L. Gilman's study delves into uncovering a precise type of gendered racial prejudice that connects black female bodies to sexual deviancy. In analysing the 'association of the black with concupiscence'[9] he posits, by examining nineteenth-century French and Viennese literature and painting, that within bourgeois society, black females came to be associated with all manner of improper lascivious behaviour including prostitution and lesbianism. The correlation between black females and overt sexuality would come to dominate the stereotypes of black women in the collective consciousness. As Kobena Mercer explains in relation to the image of the oversexed black male, the implication is that 'defined in their very *being* as sexual and nothing but sexual, [black bodies are] hence hypersexual'.[10] The positioning of the models on all fours underscores the animalistic associations conflated with elements of the sexual. Like animals pursuing the fulfilment of their base needs, the models have been posed in manners equally predatory and sexually available. Rather than providing irony, the photographic styling and staging of *Afrodizzyaction* projects on to white females a primitive core of blackness via particular recourse to jungle sexuality.

Homi Bhaba has stated that, 'An important feature of post-colonial discourse is its dependence on the concept of "fixity" in the ideological construction of otherness.'[11] With reference to the photographic, the term 'National Geographic aesthetic' has been coined to describe certain patterns exploited in photographing 'the Other'.[12] This aesthetic is based on the premise that the Western photographic image claims to capture distant peoples in their authentic state, achieved by presenting them 'as they are'; dressed in autochthonous garb and surrounded by indigenous wares. Frequently, this aesthetic exploits the marked differences in self-presentation like the titillation of bare-breasted women or the shock of pierced or scarred flesh.

The images put forward and the postures adopted are therefore not targeted at black consumption. What is then constructed are images of the Other that reflect back to the genius of the stylist, photographer and/ or fashion show director for their capture, but never to the Other or the community from which she hails.[13] Abigail Solomon-Godeau notes that difference and distance are together mobilised to produce desirability.[14] The mystique of black body language, seen as an experience remote from white culture, creates a 'narrative ... that mobilizes powerful psychological fantasies about difference and otherness, both sexual and racial'.

In Franco Rubartelli's photographs, the German model Veruschka is alternately imaged as the Great White Hunter, the hunted prey, and the exotic native woman. As the hunter, Veruschka is dressed in Yves Saint Laurent's revealing lace-up interpretation of the traditional khaki coloured, multi-pocketed hunting top, standing seductively with a rifle slung across her shoulders. The 'hunted prey' is visualised wearing animal print catsuits, stalking things unseen in the grasses of the savannah or stretched gingerly along tree branches, as would a jungle cat.

The transformation into 'exotic native' is accomplished by deploying several codes at once. The model remains dressed in gowns and swimwear by the top couturiers of the day but the selection of accessories is designed to render her as one of the largely unseen African 'they'. The hardened gourds used to carry water upon the head, the poison-tipped spears, the baskets of grain and the flaming torches fashioned from bundles of dry brush are all designed to be interpreted by the reader as the model's genuine occupation of and integration into the African spaces. The implication is that she has learned the ways of the Africans and has come to know how to manipulate their tools. 'The interest lies in the fact that the objects are accepted inducers of associations of ideas (bookcase =

intellectual)'.[15] In this case, the association is formed by spear = savage, lack of running water = primitive. In these images, the model is 'going native'.[16] Added to the deliberate placement and use of props is written commentary said to be by Veruschka herself, accompanying each photograph and followed by her signature – a further attempt to authenticate the experience captured in the pages:

> At daybreak, I went down [in Christian Dior] with the women to the Oubangui River, on the frontier of the Congo and the Central African Republic to get water.[17]
>   ... thus I began to sense the feel of each rustling blade of grass, of each gust of hot air and I set off hunting in the savannah in fringed buckskin blouse and trousers ... I even trained wielding the poisoned spear in the dress seen below.[18]

In the few pages Paul Jobling devotes to considerations of representations of the Other, he considers a fashion editorial written by Polly Devlin and photographed by Alex Chatelain for the May 1980 issue of British *Vogue*. He concludes that 'the verbal rhetoric of the piece, which, in the name of Fashion, serves to contrast civilisation and exclusivity with collective primitivism'[19] ultimately seeks to define whiteness in contrast to Otherness. The same can be said of Rubartelli's double-issue fashion story. The cultural tourism is rendered most effective by the use of a white model. In his book *White*, Richard Dyer contends that the definition of whiteness allows for variety and resists essentialism. There is an

> invisibility of whiteness as a racial position in white (which is to say dominant) discourse ... Whites are everywhere in representation. Yet precisely because of this and their placing as norm they seem not to be represented to themselves as whites but as people who are variously gendered, classed, sexualised and abled. At the level of representation, in other words, whites are not of a certain race, they're just the human race'.[20]

Dyer's claim is remarkably supported in 'Une Beauté Sauvage', one of the smaller editorials that comprise Rubartelli's travelogue: 'I've finally reached the Pygmies ... I found them dancing in the forests some 60 km from the city of Bangui and I made up my face to look like theirs.'[21]
    All fashion models are required to be malleable, hired to become the embodiment of the desired image. It is shown to what extent race

FRANCO RUBARTELLI

JUNGLE LOOK:
UNE BEAUTÉ
SAUVAGE

..."Je parvins jusqu'aux Pygmées"...
A gauche, maillot de bain découvrant les
hanches, en Dropnyl Nylfrance laqué. Karl Lagerfeld
pour Mayogaine à la Gaminerie. ... "Je les trouvai dansant
dans les forêts à 60 km de la ville de Bangui
et je me fis leur visage"... Lisez page 130.

Veruschka

97

6.1 Veruschka, styled to 'possess the face of a Pygmy'. *Vogue* (Paris) 'Jungle Look: une aventure africaine' July–August double issue 1968: Franco Rubartelli, photographer; Veruschka, model.

is fashion's disposable plaything in the model's donning of the 'face of a Pygmy' (see Figure 6.1). Trying on the ethnic identity becomes a singular opportunity to bear the label 'black' without consequence: it can be worn then removed like any of the other designer labels fitted during the excursion. The lack of essentialising characteristics to do with whiteness extends to its members the privilege of sampling essences of other cultures, while simultaneously being positioned above the effect of racism – they can, therefore, experience the coloured surface of race without having to 'feel' its more profound social impact.[22] The visual codes used to signal the tribal transformation into Pygmy – face paint, volumised hair and braided rope – are the same as those activated to amplify Veruschka's leonine attributes in an antecedent photograph. Further, the stylised expanse of black and white eye make-up, listed in the credits as having been co-created by Veruschka herself, is employed on the cover of the magazine to transform the model into a panther. As such, the native tribeswoman is conflated in the reader's mind's eye with the indigenous animal population. No attempt is made to differentiate the allure of the African villages and the bodies that inhabit them from that of the safari excursions on the plains.

Veruschka's various conversions into hunter, hunted and tribes-woman are to a very great degree mobilised by her whiteness, contained in her ability as a white person to be defined and redefined rather than categorised. She is thus able to simulate Pygmy face painting, to suggest the lustre of black skin in sunlight by being covered in gold greasepaint, to wear the braided hairstyle of the Bamara village women, to undergo myriad racialised transformations while remaining ever secure in her whiteness.

Photographer Norman Parkinson travelled to Africa with his wife for a British *Vogue* assignment, resulting in January 1969's 'Ethiopia, the land of the lion'. Wenda Parkinson's written description, together with Norman Parkinson's images, present to the *Vogue* reader a type of foreign correspondent's report from a human safari. Wenda Parkinson writes of being 'tantalised' by the discovery of 'the land of She and other beautiful creatures'.[23] In the images, the white fashion model is attended by Ethiopian women and children. In most of the images, the white model is the central figure and the indigenous people are used as authenticating background props (see Figure 6.2). Willis and Williams note that within this genre of image-making, black female bodies become 'highly orna-mental commodities … so highly aestheticized as to be fetish images – as many fashion photographs are'.[24]

Their dark skin, woven baskets, jewellery and textiles signal that the

Vogue reader has been transported elsewhere. Often the attention of the Africans is lavished on the fashion model. According to bell hooks,

> The world of fashion has also come to understand that selling products is heightened by the exploitation of Otherness … Often [indigenous peoples'] faces are blurred by the camera, a strategy which ensures that the readers will not become more enthralled by the images of Otherness than those of whiteness. The point of this photographic attempt at defamiliarization is to distance us from whiteness, so that we will return to it more intently.[25]

In Parkinson's images, the positioning of the Africans identifies the model as the central figure by paddling her down a stream, encircling her as if taking protective measures, finger combing her hair or adorning her with flowers, beads and bangles. In these images, there is a dual Otherness: the Ethiopians are represented as people with an enduring and incomprehensible mystique. Wenda Parkinson writes that she 'tried to understand and failed'.[26] Conversely, surrounded by dark, differently dressed bodies, the white model becomes defamiliarised and could be interpreted as Ethiopia's Other. In this context, her beauty, conventional in Western settings, becomes imbued with an exotic mystique of its own. The Ethiopian women smile and gaze upon her, Queen-like, as they groom her golden hair and place rings upon her fingers. Her beauty thus takes on the dimension it never has on the model's home soil.

The West's fascination with the Masai people of East Africa has been described as an 'unhappy love affair'. Perhaps to call it an unrequited love affair is more accurate. During the colonial enterprises of the Western European nations in East Africa, the Masai people were steadfast in their resistance. They would have no part of negotiations, assimilation schemes, or material incentives. They remain to this day at odds with the Kenyan government for their independent cattlemen's way of life. This seems to have made their appeal all the more profound. Their

6.2 The original *Vogue* caption reads as follows: 'The panther [below], a black cire catsuit zipped to the neck; by Simon Massey, 9½ gns, at Way In, London, Manchester. Black chiffon veil, by Ascher. Gauntlets, 59s. 6d., at Liberty. Plaited black wig from Vidal Sassoon. All sizes, colours, see Stockists. This photograph was taken at Gambela. The Annuak tribe lives in thatched cottages on the banks of the Baro river, the women are tall and slim, wear brilliant beads in necklaces and headbands.' *Vogue* (UK) 'Ethiopia, the Land of the Lion', January 1969: Norman Parkinson, photographer; model(s) unknown.

turned to Ethiopia and her kingdom of Axum, she gave birth to his child, one of the first great Emperors, Menelek, from whom HIM Haile Selassie claims descent. To see a cere-

dance, silver Maracas in their hand, drums beating and acolytes wailing, to see the etched proud faces of the high priests under their embroidered, fringed (*continued overleaf*)

brilliant in blue, pink and gold: this celebration and wedding costume is local to Harrar and consists with silver and amber and marigolds. Lipstick, Goya's Lipsheen Amber. The panther, *above*, a black resistance to assimilation and cultural cooperation, their distance from Western standards, has rendered the Masai more 'authentic' than their more cooperative countrymen. An aspect of this perceived authenticity lies in the belief that the Masai have not given in, have not in any way changed or evolved: 'an important feature of colonial discourse is its dependence on the concept of "fixity" in the ideological construction of otherness'.[27] Lynn Procter inadvertently validates Bhabha's argument by adopting a particularly Western essentialised vision of Masai culture, wherein Western modernity is positioned against the perceived animalistic primitivism of the Masai:

> These Kenyan Masai have not suffered the same stylistic repression as their fellow tribesmen in Tanzania, who have been stripped of their tribal costume. Instead the Masai of Kenya are protected like an endangered species, preserved as if in aspic and serving, like many American Indian tribes, as a tourist attraction. [The Masai are] as a living museum of photographic models.[28]

Procter posits that the white fashion models who are often on location with Masai tribes for fashion assignments offer 'a truer and more natural reflection of reality'[29] in that they echo a visibly evolving and changing way of life. The concept of the white consumption of black cultures is vividly illustrated by Procter's word choice 'preserved as if in aspic'. The savoury jelly often holds meats in a translucent edible cast. This comparison renders the existence of Masai tribes a mass of artfully designed moulded black flesh, waiting to be consumed.

Photographers have experimented with different cultures and races in the hope of enlivening the magazine pages by capturing an authentic and exciting essence. The visualisation of 'authentic' black culture will be examined via constructions of two of its most potent stereotypes: associations with the jungle and the ghetto established within commercial photography. That blackness is connected to an exotic lived experience, be it in an African village or urban environment; it must be acknowledged that each location is also the source of a potent derisive epithet. Not unlike Enoch Powell who attacked assimilationist black immigrants just as he did those who were more resistant to English acculturation, the racial insults 'jungle bunny' and 'porch monkey' target their recipients as unwelcome and somehow ill-fitting members of society. In 'jungle bunny', the timid woodside creature is made to contrast with the tropical habitat of more treacherous beasts. As for 'porch monkey', the slur originated with the gathering of blacks on the stoops and porches in front of their residences, an undesirable congregation to prejudiced whites. The monkey, since the first Darwinian and phrenological studies were undertaken, has offensively come to signify persons of the African diaspora. Again, the negative characterisation of blackness is accomplished through links with the animalistic.

Regardless of the imagery's origins, photographers have recourse to these two geographical devices as a visual cipher for authentic black experience. 'Are not the formulas of "originality" and "authenticity" in ethnic discourse a palpable legacy of European romanticism? How is the illusion of ethnic "authenticity" stylistically created?'[30]

In structuring a framework for black authenticity, 1960s fashion photographers most frequently sought an authentic vision of blackness in the land- and townscapes of Africa. Photographers like Parkinson and Rubartelli would use African scenery as ethnic surround, depicting the 'white model standing up with the natives'.[31]

> The colonized is elevated above his jungle status in proportion to his adoption of the mother country's [which is to say the colonial power's] cultural standards. He becomes whiter as he renounces his blackness, his jungle.[32]

In Fanon's estimation, the 'jungle' as a location and 'blackness' as a state of being are conflated in Western perception. Art director Jean-Paul Goude, like Procter's Masai pronouncements, sustains Fanon's assessment when recounting a project with a former girlfriend, model Toukie Smith: 'my fantasies definitely had nothing to do with hers. I saw her as this primitive, voluptuous girl-horse. She preferred champagne, caviar, and the life you see in the pages of *Vogue*.'[33] In Goude's retelling, his concept of instinctive blackness sharply contrasted his model's studied and refined self-image.

> Blacks and I were drawn to each other for some of the same reasons but to different ends. The politics of Black Power didn't interest me much ... My enthusiasm was aesthetic. Whatever the reason, most blacks then were interested in Africa, *their* interpretation of Africa, but so was I![34]

From their differing positions, Fanon and Goude, perhaps an unlikely theoretical pair, each interpret blackness as indelibly rooted to the jungle.[35] Fanon reads blackness-as-jungle in terms of a cultural imposition formed in the West. Goude's construal is the imaginary manifestation resulting from that imposition. This gives rise to asking whose version of authenticity, whose perspective is being privileged in the definition of blackness? '"Authenticity" is achieved not by some purist, archival, or preservationist attitude toward a fixed past but by a remarkable openness toward the ability of a specific idiom to interact with "outside" signals and to incorporate them.'[36]

For Werner Sollors, Professor of African-American studies, notions of the authentic update themselves by absorbing any mutations in cultural signification. These changes 'as elements of a widely shared everyday life ... become "natural" and even central elements in the vernacular'.[37] This concept of a changing ethnic authenticity contrasts with Mercer's, which sees ethnic stereotypes as a type of petrifaction where 'stereotypes [are] a fixed way of seeing that freezes the flux of experience'.[38] The coinage of authenticity has shifted from a single-point essentialised authenticity located somewhere in a timeless African construct, to an increasingly pluralistic vision of many authenticities.

Where once Africa was viewed through the lens of Joseph Conrad's Belgian Congo, the dangerous 'heart of darkness' not to be entered, the off-limits urban centres have come to replace cultural tourism with gentrification of style. Like discourses exposing the 'male gaze', is it possible to subscribe to a belief in the artificial creation of the black authentic? Feminist film theorist Laura Mulvey argues that women have been socialised to apply the male gaze, learning to view images of other females through the same sexualised and objectifying lens as do men. Are blacks thus acculturated to read representations of black people in the same sexualised, objectified, stereotyped manner as presented to white people? Are black interpretations all mediated through a degree of the 'white gaze' or is something entirely other seen and felt? bell hooks distinguishes between cultural appropriation and cultural appreciation. She suggests that if we acknowledge the ways that the desire for pleasure, and that includes erotic longings, inform our politics and our understanding of difference, 'we may know better how desire disrupts, subverts, and makes resistance possible. We cannot, however accept these new images uncritically.'[39]

If this is so, what are the possibilities for the commercial photographer? Are image-makers 'strait-jacketed' into representing certain images by established codes? Can they negotiate irony and varied experience within the highly codified medium of fashion photography? Can any small successes be gauged within the expansion of the visual language? Can or do Vogue readers – black and white – abstract from the portrayals of authenticity in order to extrapolate the theoretical changes the construct has undergone? Indeed, Stuart Hall has commented

> Popular culture, commodified and stereotyped as it often is, is not at all, as we sometimes think of it, the arena where we find who we really are, the truth of our experience. It is an arena that is *profoundly* mythic. It is a theatre of popular desires, a theatre of popular fantasies. It is where we discover and play with the identifications of ourselves, where we are imagined, where we are represented, not only to the audiences out there who do not get the message, but to ourselves for the first time.[40]

The use of stereotypes, what Roland Barthes calls 'ready play with the supposed knowledge of its readers', enables a magazine to convey a vast quantity of information relying on few complex visual cues.[41] Jonathan de Villiers photographed the editorial 'Ngong Hills Kenya' for Vogue Italia in April 2002. Though the intent was to subvert the 'African Other' aesthetic espoused by Parkinson and Rubartelli, it is affirmed. In one image, an African woman kneels at model Erin O'Connor's feet, assuming the Mammy role, wearing a striped maid's dress with eyelet trim and worn moccasins. The activation of specific sartorial codes and body language – one figure crouched down with head bowed and one figure personified only through confident stance and expensive shoes – signal the domesticity and subservience of the African woman in contrast to the self-assured, worldly opulence of the 'mistress'. In reproducing the codes used by Parkinson and Rubartelli, de Villiers, too, visualises Young's conclusion that '[the black woman] serves as the other of others'.[42]

'In examining mythic speech, it is necessary not only to describe its concrete manifestations, but also to attend to its silences, its absences, its omissions. For what is not spoken – what is unspeakable, mystified or occulted – turns always on historical as well as psychic repressions'.[43]

When it comes to carrying out work which involves representations of black people, the analysis of images has a heightened political inflection, since representations of black people are always deemed to 'mean' something, to be laden with symbolism in regard to 'race' in racially stratified societies.[44]

Unmasking the visual tactics used to illustrate latent ideological constructs must rely on the dual processes of injecting political readings while uncovering others that might be deliberately 'built into' the image. Fashion images do not easily move beyond the confines of stereotype. Even when the messages are not deliberate, there is ever a racial element because the images are constructed so as to reinforce perceptions of blacks' position in society, conceptions of black attractiveness and notions of black culture in general. It is precisely because codified and commodified stereotypes propagate beliefs in a true and 'authentic' black experience visualised in fashion media that its silences must be attended to.

> Despite civil rights struggle, the 1960s' black power movement, and the power slogans like 'black is beautiful' masses of black people continue to be socialized *via* mass media and non-progressive educational systems to internalize white supremacist thoughts and values.[45]

The fashion industry, as a 'culture industry', appropriates the political in culture in order to create arresting images.[46] Visualisation always takes place with a background of economic considerations. Through the process of appropriation and assimilation, the fashion industry necessarily depoliticises its sources. It stands proud, rather, affirming that it is never political, historical nor analytical. In the end, however, a fashion magazine seeks so aggressively to be perpetually current that it will attest very clearly to certain historical and political referents of its time.

> We saw that the code of connotation was in all likelihood neither 'natural' nor 'artificial' but historical, or, if it be preferred, 'cultural'. Its signs are gestures, attitudes, expressions, colours or effects, endowed with certain meanings by virtue of the practice of a certain society: the link between signifier and signified remains if not unmotivated, at lest entirely historical ... Thanks to its code of connotation the reading of the photograph is thus always historical; it depends on the reader's 'knowledge' just as though it were a matter of a real language, intelligible only if one has learned the signs.[47]

The fashion publication industry, trading in the currency of image, depends on a particular language of codes and signs. It cannot remain exempt from accountability for its racial (and by extension, other) politics. In particular, *Vogue's* prominent positionality as purveyor of contemporary visual culture requires that its political stance – often professing to be apolitical – be questioned.

Notes

1 Based on original research contained in my unpublished MA dissertation, Z. Whitley, *Funky Afro Chicks: Charting Representations of Blackness in Vogue, 1966–2002* (V&A/RCA, 2003).

2 T. Wolfe, *Radical Chic and Mau-Mauing the Flak Catchers* (London: Picador, 2002, first published 1970), p. 5.

3 *Black Panther* (Oakland, California: 20 July 1967).

4 K. Mercer, *Welcome to the Jungle: New Positions in Black Cultural Studies* (London: Routledge, 1994), p. 107.

5 Mercer, *Welcome to the Jungle*, p. 107.

6 M. Leeds Craig, *Ain't I a Beauty Queen: Black Women, Beauty, and the Politics of Race* (London: Oxford University Press, 2002), p. 156.

7 B. Anderson, *Imagined Communities* (London: Fontana Press, 1983).

8 Lola Young and Paul Gilroy have each noted this perceived social necessity. Young, in *Fear of the Dark* (London: Routledge, 1996) has written, 'Differences are constructed through the process of creating distinct categorizations which assist in the production and maintenance of an illusory order in a chaotic and fragmented world', p. 32. Gilroy explains racial categorisation as a type of wayward cultural compass whereby race 'punctuates denial, displacement and boredom of national decline by focusing on prejudice', see P. Gilroy, 'Has It Come to This?' lecture at Tate Modern, London, 2003.

9 S. Gilman, *Difference and Pathology* (Ithaca: Cornell University Press, 1985), p. 79.

10 Mercer, *Welcome to the Jungle*, p. 174.

11 H. Bhaba, 'The Other Question: the Stereotype and Colonial Discourse', in Jessica Evans and Stuart Hall, *Visual Culture: The Reader* (London and Milton Keynes: Open University and Sage, 1999), pp. 370–378.

12 D. Willis and C. Williams, *The Black Female Body: A Photographic History* (Philadelphia: Temple University Press, 2002).

13 'The experience of the primitive or of the primitive artefact is, therefore,

and among other things, valued as an aid to creation, and to the act of genius located in the artist's exemplary act of recognition' (see A. Solomon-Godeau in N. Broude and M. Garrard, *The Expanding Discourse* (New York: IconEditions, 1992), p. 315. Agency lies with the 'artist-as-genius' for identifying the Other. At best, the Other might be attributed the title 'muse' but possesses no agency of her own.

14 Solomon-Godeau, *The Expanding Discourse*, p. 314.

15 R. Barthes, *Image-Music-Text*, translated and edited by Stephen Heath (Glasgow: Fontana, 1977), p. 22.

16 P. Jobling, *Fashion Spreads* (London: Berg, 1999), p. 78; see also Solomon-Godeau.

17 *Vogue* (Paris: July–August 1968).

18 *Vogue* (Paris: July–August 1968).

19 Jobling, *Fashion Spreads*, p. 78.

20 R. Dyer, *White* (London: Routledge, 1997), p. 3.

21 *Vogue* (Paris: July–August 1968).

22 See Nirmal Puwar's 'Multicultural fashion ...' on the appropriation of South Asian 'ethnic' items: 'The capacity of white bodies to play with bindhies and mendhies while retaining the pleasure of whiteness as universal point is a "disavowed, inverted, self-reverential form of racism" built on ... "the multiculturalist respect for Other's specificity [as] the very norm of asserting one's own superiority"', p. 76.

23 See British *Vogue* (January 1969).

24 Willis and Williams, *The Black Female Body* (Philadelphia: Temple University Press, 2002), pp. 81–82.

25 b. hooks, *Black Looks* (Toronto: Between the Lines, 1992), pp. 28–29.

26 See British *Vogue* (January 1969).

27 H. Bhabha, 'The Other Question', 1983: 18.

28 L. Procter, *Fashion & Anti-Fashion* (London: Cox & Wyman, 1978), p. 28.

29 Procter, *Fashion & Anti-Fashion*, p. 28.

30 W. Sollors, 'The Idea of Ethnicity' in W. T. Anderson (ed.), *The Fontana Post-Modernism Reader* (London: Fontana, 1996), p. 59.

31 Zoé Whitley interview with Armet Francis, 2003.

32 F. Fanon, *Black Skin, White Masks* (London: Pluto, 1986), pp. 18 and 33.

33 J. P. Goude, *Jungle Fever* (1981), pp. 40–41.

34 Goude, *Jungle Fever*, p. 31.

35 Goude distinguishes his European 'romantic conception of blackness' from

the more rigidly defined notions of white Americans: 'As a European, let me pause here to say, I have the advantage of being able to describe my romantic conception of blackness from a white point of view. My conception is free of all social connotations because I am European. Americans cannot dissociate themselves from the social implications of their artistic evaluation of black people. Liberals are afraid of being mistaken for flippant, superficial or frivolous in this kind of artistic evaluation. As for racist conservatives, of course, their artistic evaluation is nil to begin with. They are so busy thinking of blacks as parasites of American society they can't even think of them seriously in terms of artistic implication. So, I really find myself in a strange situation, because on the one hand liberals are embarrassed by my attitude, while racists ironically misinterpret me as one of them. And the blacks? I'm not sure; I think my conception may appeal to some with a sensibility similar to mine. I'm not sure ...' (Goude, *Jungle Fever*, p. 107).

36 Sollors in Anderson, *The Fontana Postmodernism Reader*, p. 60.

37 Sollors in Anderson, *The Fontana Postmodernism Reader*, p. 60.

38 Mercer, *Welcome to the Jungle*, p. 174.

39 hooks, *Black Looks*, p. 39.

40 S. Hall. 'What is this Black in Black Popular Culture?' in D. Morley and K.-H. Chen, *Stuart Hall* (London: Routledge, 1996), p. 74.

41 Barthes, *Image-Music-Text*, p. 27.

42 L. Young, 'Missing Persons: Fantasising Black Women in *Black Skin, White Masks*' in A. Read, *The Fact of Blackness* (London: ICA, 1996), p. 100.

43 Solomon-Godeau, *The Expanding Discourse*, p. 314.

44 Young, *Fear of the Dark*, p. 1.

45 hooks in *Black Looks*, p. 18.

46 See Susan Sontag's *On Photography* (London: Allen Lane, 1978) for a discussion of 'the interesting' and cliché as photographic devices.

47 Barthes, *Image-Music-Text*, pp. 27–28.

Part III
Promoting design through magazines

Since the inception of mass-circulation titles, the belief in the persuasive power of magazines, although still not proven scientifically, explains the considerable investment in their appearance. Publishers and advertisers alike have recognised the appeal of high-quality illustrations to potential readers. By their nature, magazines form an ideal representational medium through which to discern the characteristics of objects and to offer advice and discrimination about consumer choice. The following essays concentrate on a genre of magazine that developed from the 1870s, devoted to the discussion of design interests, information and selling. They analyse the presentation of modern design and craft ideals, to explore the editorial and design strategies employed. The first essay examines the origins of prescriptive literature in the late-nineteenth century. In particular, it analyses the inter-relationship between books and magazines and explores the nature and source of their illustrations, which involved transatlantic exchange. In the second, which is a discussion between a former designer and editor of *Design* magazine, the particular character of British Modernism in the 1950s and 1960s is revealed. As a publicly-funded magazine, *Design* represented an attempt to define a new role for design journalism. The third essay, which is a study of *Crafts* magazine, itself also an official voice and symptom of the professionalisation of the applied arts in late-twentieth century, shows how Modernist design principles were adapted to promote postmodern content. From these studies, we come to understand how magazines can bridge the space between official discourse on taste and aesthetics, and the interests of the professional or general reader.

7 ❖ '... information for the ignorant and aid for the advancing ...': Macmillan's 'Art at Home' series, 1876–83

Emma Ferry

SOME of the best known volumes of domestic design advice published in the late-nineteenth century first appeared as magazine articles; perhaps most famously, Charles L. Eastlake's *Hints on Household Taste in Furniture, Upholstery and Other Details* (1868), was originally published in the *Cornhill Magazine* (1864) and the *Queen* (1864–66). This process occurred on both sides of the Atlantic, for instance, the series of articles on 'Beds, Tables, Stools and Candlesticks', written by the American art critic Clarence M. Cook for *Scribner's Illustrated Monthly*, were collected, rearranged and republished as *The House Beautiful* in 1877.[1] However, this change in format was not always straightforward, as is demonstrated by the production of three volumes in Macmillan's 'Art At Home' series.

Published between 1876 and 1883, the 'Art at Home' series was a collection of domestic advice manuals aimed explicitly at an expanding lower middle-class readership. Devised and edited by the Reverend W. J. Loftie, the series eventually encompassed subjects as diverse as *Amateur Theatricals* and *Sketching from Nature*. However, as sources for the design historian, arguably the most interesting of the final twelve volumes are the four books that dealt exclusively with aspects of the domestic interior. First issued between 1876 and 1878, Rhoda and Agnes Garrett's *Suggestions for House Decoration* (1876), Mrs Orrinsmith's *The Drawing Room* (1877), Mrs Loftie's *The Dining Room* (1878) and Lady Barker's *The Bedroom and Boudoir* (1878), offered a range of advice based on both professional and personal experiences.

These books and their illustrations are mentioned in almost every study that considers the late nineteenth-century domestic interior, where they have been interpreted as indicators of how people furnished their rooms during the late-1870s.[2] Nonetheless, many writers have missed the value of the 'Art at Home' series as a set of cultural documents: Mark Girouard, for example, simply dismissed it as 'a very superficial series of little books, aimed at the popular market'.[3] However, research into the production of series suggests that the significance of these texts is precisely all that Girouard has rejected. The advice offered was elementary, but these 'little books' were far from superficial. Instead, they should be interpreted as a complex collection of discourses, which revealed contemporary concerns with what Nicola Humble has identified as 'new constructions of class, revised gender roles and relations, regional and national identities, history, economics and the momentous clash between science and religion'.[4]

Unravelling the complex relationship between the 'Art at Home' series and a range of contemporary magazines, in terms of its production and its reception, this essay charts the publication of the books and highlights the difficulties of using them as conventional sources of information about the Victorian interior. In particular, this essay focuses on the images used to illustrate the 'Art at Home' series, which had been previously published in a magazine and appeared concurrently in an American book. It suggests that while this may have resulted in a transatlantic exchange of aesthetic ideas, it also raised issues surrounding copyright.

The production of the series can be traced through the correspondence collated in the *General Letterbooks* and other collections of letters held in the Macmillan Archive.[5] This correspondence has been used to construct a narrative that recounts the publication of the 'Art at Home' series. These letters revealed the initial plan for the series, recorded the commissioning of authors, illustrators, engravers and bookbinders, and charted the progress of the volumes as they were written or, in some cases, remained unwritten. They also provided an insight into the marketing techniques employed, mentioned the reviews that appeared in a wide range of journals, and gave a sense of the overall success of the venture.

In March 1876, following discussions with a representative from the American publishing house, Coates & Co, of Philadelphia, W. J. Loftie wrote to Alexander Macmillan, co-founder of Macmillan & Co, outlining his scheme for an entire series of small 'Art at Home' books. Aimed at a readership composed of 'people of moderate or small income', initially, this joint venture was to comprise eight books; four to be written in England and four in America, all of which would be published by Coates.[6] The four British volumes (which it seems had already been commissioned and in some cases were nearing completion) were described briefly. They included Loftie's own contribution to the series initially entitled *Art at Home*; Rhoda and Agnes Garrett's *House Decoration*; and two other volumes (that were never published) called *Good Things We Have Lost*: or *Hints from Old English Households* and, *Hints from Foreign Households*.[7] Loftie proposed that Macmillan should publish these four books but not the four unnamed American volumes which he felt 'would be of little or no use here: as the subjects proposed were such as would require local treatment'.[8] Instead, he wanted Macmillan to commission at least four more books, including *Art at Table* and *Dress*, while proposing J. J. Stevenson for a volume on *Domestic Architecture* and John Hullah to write on *Music at Home*.[9] Loftie recommended that the books should be octavo, approximately 150 pages long and illustrated with relatively cheap photozincographs. He suggested that the authors should receive £30 or £40 for their copyright, though naturally, the better-known authors would receive more money for their work, and he thought that the books should sell for a shilling (the equivalent of £3 today), which corresponded to the price of 25 cents proposed by Coates. Having volunteered to oversee the whole project in return for 4 per cent on the retail price, Loftie naturally sought to expand the series even further. He wrote:

> The list of eight subjects given above by no means exhausts those of which I have thought. Miss Plues could do a very pretty book on Gardening. Another of the series might be on Needlework & Embroidery, generally, another on Sketching from Nature, another on Carving & amateur Carpentry; even reading aloud & elocution would make one, as well as dancing & gymnastics. Art would however be kept strictly in view, & the general title of the series would be *Art at Home*.[10]

Alexander Macmillan expressed doubts 'about the *serial* form' of the scheme being more inclined to think one book would have been better, as he thought: 'The subjects so topple over into each other.'[11] Eventually,

7.1 A comparison of the British and American front covers of Macmillan's 'Art at Home' series.

however, Macmillan & Co. were to publish twelve volumes as the 'Art at Home' series.

Planned as a collectable set, from the outset the series was given a clear visual identity (see Figure 7.1). The British books were bound in a suitably 'artistic' blue-grey cloth, bearing the title, the authors' names and the Macmillan initial engraved by J. D. Cooper.[12] The four American volumes eventually published by Porter & Coates were bound in brown cloth and decorated with the 'Art at Home' motif designed by Harry Soane.[13] This motif, which is signed and dated '1876' by Soane, appeared on the title page of both the British and American books (Figure 7.2).

This outward visual unity belies the diverse and often contradictory advice given by the contributing authors: each volume was written as a distinct text that highlighted its own concerns and scarcely related to

7.2 The 'Art at Home' series motif designed by Harry Soane c.1876.

others in the series. This discrepancy was noted by the *Saturday Review* when the first two books were issued:

> Mr. Loftie has a leaning towards drawing-room papers with no patterns, and towards painted or panelled dining rooms. But if one turns from his manual to Miss Garrett's – and it is to be remarked that these works belong to the same series, and are bound in cloth of the same tint, 'the bluest of things grey and the greyest of things blue' – there is a fresh perplexity. The dining room paper in Miss Garrett's design is not plain but laid out in large squares, interlaced with the leaves and flowers of some unknown specimens of the vegetable creation.[14]

The final twelve books that formed the British series fell into several groups. Historians have tended to focus on the moral aspect of William Loftie's *A Plea for Art in the House*, which, after all, was subtitled *'with*

special reference to the economy of collecting works of art, and the importance of taste in education and morals'. The religious sentiment expressed
in his final chapter certainly served to remind the reader that Loftie
was an Anglican clergyman; moreover, given the links between the
religious revival and design reform, this was the part of Loftie's book
that has received most attention from twentieth-century design historians. However, addressing male readers, much of Loftie's treatise, like
Andrew Lang's *The Library*, is largely concerned with connoisseurship
and the long-term financial benefits of collecting as a form of investment. Margaret Oliphant's *Dress*, John Hullah's *Music in the House*
and the Pollocks' *Amateur Theatricals* offered historical information on
these subjects, which suggested suitable forms of appearance, behaviour
and entertainment in the home for lower-middle-class aspirants. Other
volumes, including Charles G. Leland's *The Minor Arts*, Elizabeth Glaist-
er's *Needlework*, and Tristram J. Ellis's *Sketching from Nature*, can best be
classified as instruction manuals, which gave detailed descriptions of the
techniques used in a variety of decorative arts and crafts.

The contributing authors form an interesting group of subject
specialists and writers, and while some of them, notably Mrs Oliphant
and Lady Barker, had professional associations with Macmillan, others
seem to be personal acquaintances and colleagues of Loftie. William
Loftie is an interesting figure, with a surprisingly substantial entry in the
Dictionary of National Biography. Born in Tandraghee, County Armagh in
July 1839, Loftie graduated from Trinity College, Dublin, in 1862. In
1865 he took holy orders and in the same year he married the widowed
Martha Jane Burnett (née Anderson). Loftie served three curacies before
becoming assistant chaplain at the Chapel Royal, Savoy, in 1871, where
he remained until retiring in 1895. Managing to combine his clerical
duties with journalism, Loftie 'wrote voluminously in periodicals'.[15]
He contributed to the SPCK's *People's Magazine* (1867–73) and was
appointed editor in 1872. It is here that he published illustrations by
Kate Greenaway, having bought the first drawings that she sold publicly
after their exhibition at the Dudley Gallery in 1868. Loftie is also credited with having advised Greenaway to 'devote her energies solely to the
illustration of children's books':[16] several of her illustrations appeared in
volumes from the 'Art at Home' series. Loftie worked for a range of journals, writing for the Church of England newspaper, the *Guardian* between

1870 and 1876, and joining the staff of the *Saturday Review* in 1874 and of the *National Observer* in 1894. Loftie's numerous publications reflected his antiquarian interests, many of them covering aspects of archaeology, art and architecture; and while he wrote fourteen books on the history of London, he is also known for editing the *Orient Line Guide for Travellers* and his studies of Egyptian artefacts. Loftie's literary connections, wide-ranging artistic and archaeological interests and membership of organisations and clubs, such as the Savile and the SPAB, meant he was ideally placed to recruit suitable authors.[17]

The first two books in the series, Loftie's *A Plea for Art in the House* and the Garretts' *Suggestions for House Decoration*, were both published in November 1876. The Garretts' book was based on a paper entitled 'How to Improve the Interior of Modern Houses', which Rhoda Garrett had presented at the Social Science Congress in 1876: it was later published in *The Transactions of the National Association for the Promotion of Social Science* and in *Macmillan's Magazine*.[18] A letter from Alexander Macmillan to Rhoda Garrett indicated the marketing methods employed in promoting the series, which was based wholly on successful reviews of the books in a wide range of magazines and newspapers:

> We have already sent a copy to Mr S. C. Hale of the *Art Journal* & I have instructed our clerk to offer him clichés of any of the illustrations for insertion in his paper along with any review he may have. The *Building News* has borrowed some. Copies were sent to two Manchester, two Birmingham, two Liverpool and one Leeds paper, also to the *Scotsman* & *Glasgow Herald*. Altogether we sent about 60 copies all over the country.[19]

Reviews for the first two volumes have been located in national and provincial newspapers, trade journals and the architectural press. On the whole they were favourable, and the comments of the London *Examiner* were reproduced in later editions:

> In these decorative days the volumes bring calm counsel and kindly suggestions, with information for the ignorant and aid for the advancing, that ought to help many a feeble, if well-meaning pilgrim along the weary road, at the end whereof, far off, lies the House Beautiful – many a pilgrim to whom otherwise the Slough of Despond and the Hill of Difficulty had been unsurmountable obstacles. If the whole series but

continues as it has begun – if the volumes yet to be rival the two initial ones, it will be beyond praise as a library of household art.[20]

It is perhaps not surprising that the review of the 'Art at Home' series appeared on the same page as a review for an edition of Bunyan's *Pilgrim's Progress*, the text that was the origin of the phrase 'House Beautiful'.

Being 'on the regular staff',[21] Loftie managed to secure a lengthy commentary in the *Saturday Review*. However, the anonymous reviewer, having highlighted examples of contradictory advice given by Loftie and the Garretts, devoted most of the review to criticising the contemporary 'decorative craze':

> Every few months we see a change in the highest decorative society; one hobby is as good as another hobby and no better. People who do not care about Queen Anne and Chippendale have their own tastes of some other sort, and do not mind being looked on as little better than the wicked. Perhaps the one great moral effect of the fashion of decoration is that it provides matter for talk as exciting as scandal, and less dangerous. When you pick a lady's curtains to pieces her character escapes criticism. To provide a harmless substitute for scandal, and to make even London houses not uninteresting to their occupants, is the office of domestic art.[22]

The reviews published by the trade and professional journals were mixed. A highly favourable review was published in the *Building News*, which amounted to five columns and included two illustrations from Rhoda and Agnes Garrett's *Suggestions for House Decoration*. However, the sarcastic and misogynistic review in the *Furniture Gazette* drew attention to inaccuracies and faults detected within the Garretts' treatise, commenting that these were errors

> such as would be made by the fair sex, who are rightly or wrongly, in the habit of looking for advice and instruction to the sterner half of creation, and of taking for granted many clever men's sayings, which they would doubt or at least question, if they came from their own sex.[23]

The Macmillan Archive reveals that the finished plates of the first two volumes were shipped across the Atlantic in November 1876 to the American publishers, who were at liberty to publish the books in 'another form if desired'.[24] Subsequently, reviews also appeared in American journals: the four American books carried excerpts of reviews published in various journals, including *The North American, The American Builder* and the *Church's Musical Visitor*. A lengthy review traced in *The American Architect and Building News* in May 1877 commented on the inappropriate nature of English advice for American readers.

> The principles of taste as laid down in these books, though elementary, are in the main sound and of useful application anywhere, but in some respects they seem better suited to the atmosphere of London than our own … We Americans may continue to rejoice in our contrasts of positive and neutral colours, and, under our clear skies, to profit by the purity and freshness of bright walls.[25]

The reviewer also criticised the illustrations to Loftie's volume: 'We must protest too against the woodcuts in Mr Loftie's book, which certainly do more harm than good; that on p. 38 especially we might select as an example to be avoided in every respect of subject and execution.'[26]

The illustrations commissioned or chosen for the 'Art at Home' series can also be identified through correspondence in the Macmillan Archive. Prominent suffragists, Rhoda and Agnes Garrett were trained interior designers who ran a successful house decorating business from their Gower Street home, creating fashionable Queen Anne style interiors.[27] The Macmillan Archive shows that they had produced their own illustrations for *House Decoration*, which included several of their own furniture designs and decorative schemes.[28] However, the other three volumes that also dealt with the domestic interior were illustrated in a far more complex manner, as Mrs Haweis revealed in her stinging criticism of the series:

> I vainly overhauled the many manuals of good advice now daily pouring from the press – among them *'House Decoration'* in the Art at Home series – a series, by the way, which, considering how good was the primal notion, has been ill-carried out by the writers, and is meagre in suggestions to a miracle. Not a hint for the real beautifying of stoves, nor of the house inside or out, was to be found, save the time worn command to destroy mirrors and have 'Queen Anne' fenders; and the illustrations, which are peculiarly American in character, better suited the articles in *'Scribner's Illustrated Monthly'*, where they first appeared, than the English series, which they probably fettered.[29]

The illustrations, many by Inglis, Sandier and Lathrop, were indeed taken from 'Beds and Tables, Stools and Candlesticks', the series of eleven illustrated articles on house furnishing written by Clarence M. Cook. Originally appearing in *Scribner's Monthly* between June 1875 and May 1877, the first article opened thus:

> There never was a time when so many books written for the purpose of bringing the subject of architecture – its history, its theories, its practice – down to the level of the popular understanding, were produced as in this time of ours. And, from the house itself, we are now set to thinking and theorizing about the dress and decoration of our rooms: how best to make them comfortable and handsome; and books are written, and magazine and newspaper articles, to the end that on a matter which concerns everybody, everybody may know what s the latest word.[30]

In *Sweetness and Light*, his study of late-nineteenth century 'Queen Anne Style', Mark Girouard discussed these articles and the influence of the decorator Daniel Cottier, whose furniture designs appear in many of the illustrations and who later designed the front cover of *The House Beautiful*. Within this discussion Girouard claimed that Macmillan & Co., had plagiarised Cook's illustrations for use in the 'Art at Home' series.

This accusation of plagiarism has been repeated more recently,[31] but research has revealed that in March 1877, Cook had written to Frederick Macmillan offering him the British publication rights to his articles. Macmillan, however, after asking Loftie for his advice on the matter, was to refuse this proposal.[32] He wrote to Cook:

> I know your articles in 'Scribners' well & since your letter came have talked them over with my partners & some artistic friends. The general impression is that your papers, as they stand, would not be suitable for English sale.
>
> You can no doubt well understand that the conditions in the two countries are somewhat different, that the difficulties encountered in house finding & furnishing on the one are not those in the other, while of course there are in your articles many purely local allusions that would be meaningless to English readers. In view of these things the only plan that seems to us practical would be for us to buy the very beautiful illustrations & to re-cast or re-write the text so as to suit it to English requirements.[33]

After brief negotiations, Macmillan & Co. bought electrotypes of the original wood engravings from Scribner for £100, and immediately set about finding authors willing to write new books around the identical illustrations many of which represented furnishings displayed in Daniel Cottier's New York showroom.[34]

Before the electroplates had even crossed the Atlantic, Mrs Loftie had proposed a book entitled *The Dining Room*.[35] Letters to her husband from George Lillie Craik indicated that both Lady Barker and Mrs Orrinsmith, having been shown copies of Cook's original articles, were equally confident that they could produce suitable texts, which appeared later as *The Bedroom and Boudoir* and *The Drawing Room* respectively.[36]

These three volumes were all written and published, complete with their American illustrations between 1877 and 1878, and a comparison of *The House Beautiful* with the 'Art at Home' books reveals the different approaches that Mrs Orrinsmith, Lady Barker and Mrs Loftie took when writing around these images.

Mrs Lucy Orrinsmith (née Faulkner) was a craftswoman who, with her brother Charles and younger sister Kate, had worked with William Morris, producing panels of hand-painted tiles and embroideries after designs by Burne-Jones. She was also a talented wood-engraver, having trained in the art at the office of Smith & Linton under Harvey Orrin Smith, whom she married in 1870. Mrs Orrinsmith's involvement with the 'Art at Home' series seems to be the result of a friendship with her Beckenham neighbours, George Lillie Craik, a partner in Macmillan & Co., and his wife, the novelist Dinah Mulock Craik.[37]

The *Scribner's* illustrations appeared in only six of the final eight chapters of her book on *The Drawing Room*. Mrs Orrinsmith largely resolved the difficulties of writing text round these illustrations by reorganising them, inventing new descriptions, and renaming many of the cuts. For instance, an illustration 'drawn by Mr. Lathrop, from "the life"'[38] appeared in *The House Beautiful* entitled 'A French Settee', but reappeared as 'A "Sheraton" Sofa' in *The Drawing Room*. Similarly, an 'Italian Fire-screen' described by Cook becomes 'lovely pieces of Japanese embroidery ... worked in glowing silks, representing peacocks' feathers'[39] (Figures 7.3 and 7.4) in *The Drawing Room*. It is arguable whether this says more about the knowledge of the author, the quality of the image or the fluidity of its meaning.[40]

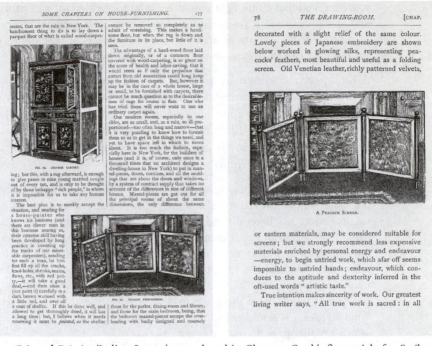

SOME CHAPTERS ON HOUSE-FURNISHING.   177

A PEACOCK SCREEN.

7.3 and 7.4 An 'Italian Screen' reproduced in Clarence Cook's first article for *Scribner's Illustrated* and later retitled a 'Peacock Screen' by Mrs Orrinsmith in *The Drawing Room*.

Mrs Orrinsmith's manipulation of image and text is best demonstrated in her chapter on 'Furniture', where in a damning critique of contemporary workmanship and popular taste, she advised her readers to 'Buy old furniture for the drawing-room'[41] and carefully arranged the woodcuts to construct an illustrated history of furniture styles. However, the reuse of the illustrations, particularly the designs by E. W. Godwin, caused criticism in the professional press. Indeed, the review in the *Building News* prompted an angry response from Macmillan, who wrote to the editor:

> Our attention has been called to a review of Mrs Orrinsmith's 'The Drawing Room' which appears in your paper of the 16th inst. In which you point to an illustration as 'taken bodily from the Building News'.
>
> We would point out to you that while the book was in the press

someone said that he thought that this cut had appeared in your paper, and Mr Loftie called at your office for the purpose of asking permission to reproduce it. He was assured there however that he was under a mistake and that the design must have been published elsewhere.[42]

A biting review written by Godwin himself also appeared in *The British Architect and Northern Engineer*. His designs, first published in the *British Architect*,[43] had also appeared in Cook's original articles and *The House Beautiful*, where, modified by Lathrop, they are at least acknowledged as his work. What Godwin condemned was their unacknowledged reproduction in the 'Art at Home' series:

> In the *Art at Home* series, Mrs Orrinsmith lecturers us on *the Drawing Room*. In her last chapter she says (p. 142), 'The encouragement of original ideas has been throughout the motive of this book.' She also trusts that certain of her readers are 'convinced that personal perseverance in the search after decorative beauty will be rewarded by results apparently unattainable except by those who have some gift of the nature of inspiration'. This is all very fine, but if Mrs Orrinsmith and her friends would have the grace to acknowledge the sources of their 'original ideas', it would enlighten readers as to the method to adopt in searching 'after pure decorative beauty'.[44]

A design for a fireplace by E. W. Godwin was also among the illustrations allocated to Lady Barker. Probably unaware of its origins in *The Architect*, Lady Barker did not acknowledge the designer. Moreover, ignoring the merits of the design, she remarked that the fireplace 'shows a pretty arrangement of picture, mirror and shelves for china':[45] one can almost hear Godwin gnashing his teeth.

The Macmillan Archive reveals that, as an established and popular writer, the Jamaican-born Lady Barker was offered £50 for suitable text to complement the electrotypes. Famous for publications that recounted her experiences of life in the colonies, including *Station Life in New Zealand* (1870), *Station Amusements in New Zealand* (1873) and *A Year's Housekeeping in South Africa* (1877), she also wrote stories for *Good Words for the Young* and reviewed books for *The Times*. In 1874, Lady Barker had become editor of the Church of England family magazine *Evening Hours*. This periodical serialised several of her books, including her 'Notes on Cooking', later collected and reissued as *First Lessons in the Principles of Cooking* (1874), which prompted her appointment as the first Lady Superintendent of Henry Cole's newly founded National School of Cookery.

The Bedroom and Boudoir was written very quickly, proposed shortly after Lady Barker's return from Natal and while she was preparing to leave England once more – this time for Mauritius, where her husband, Frederick Broome, had been appointed Colonial Secretary. Some sections of the text are clearly based on her earlier series of articles for *Evening Hours*, 'Houses and Housekeeping', particularly those on 'Bedrooms' and 'The Nursery'. However, in the passages that described the illustrations, Lady Barker also drew heavily on Cook's articles. The most glaring example concerns the description of a Japanese chest. Compare first, Cook's original text:

> No one but a man knows what a blessing this shirt-drawer is. It will hold the week's wash of shirts without tumbling or crowding, and nothing else need be allowed to usurp a place in it. In these four drawers is room for all one man's linen; and in the little closet, which contains three drawers and a hiding-place for money (which the owner did not discover until after a year's possession), there is room for all his trinkets and valuables. When the two boxes are placed together, the whole measures three feet one inch in length by three feet four high, and one foot five deep.[46]

with Lady Barker's version:

> But the male heart will be sure to delight specially in that one deep drawer for shirts, and the shallow one at the top for collars, pocket handkerchiefs, neckties, and so forth. The lower drawers would hold a moderate supply of clothes, and the little closet contains three drawers, besides a secret place for money and valuables. When the two boxes, for they are really little else, are placed side by side they measure only three feet one inch long; three feet four high, and one foot five deep.[47]

Given her colonial experiences, when the plates from Cook's articles were allocated to the authors of the 'Art at Home' series, Lady Barker was apportioned any that illustrated non-European furniture, regardless of its original placing in Cook's text. Thus, in *The Bedroom and Boudoir*, Lady Barker described a Chinese Cabinet, an Indian Screen, a Chinese sofa, and a bamboo chair 'of a familiar pattern to all travellers on the P. and O.

boats, and whose acquaintance I first made in Ceylon.'[48] All these illustrations originally appeared in Cook's chapter on *The Living Room*.

Whereas Mrs Orrinsmith made endless references to furnishings by Morris & Co., the necessity of fitting the text around the illustrations made it impossible for Lady Barker to advocate a particular style, especially when she began to write about bedroom furniture. Indeed, the review published in *The Spectator* commented on these illustrations:

> We cannot conclude without a word or two about the numerous illustrations; may of them are very inferior – and this one does not expect in a work on art – while some of them, those especially in which a figure is introduced, are quite ludicrously bad. Lady Barker herself cannot be satisfied with them, and they are most detrimental to the book, as one's eye is naturally first caught by them, in turning over the leaves. A few carefully chosen and carefully drawn subjects would have been far better in every way.[49]

The difficulty posed by the images was most apparent in her chapter fittingly entitled 'Odds and Ends of Decoration', where she managed to describe a picture stand, a bamboo sofa, a piano and 'a great deal of "rubbish" dear, perhaps, only to the owner for the sake of association'.[50] Here, before paraphrasing Cook's description of a South American pitcher, in an ironic reference to the unhappy mix of text and images, Lady Barker commented: 'The worst of such a delightful den as I am imagining, or rather describing, is the tendency of the most incongruous possessions to accumulate themselves in it as time goes on.'[51]

While the illustrations Lady Barker described had been bought from *Scribner's Illustrated Monthly*, research also shows that a chapter of *The Bedroom and Boudoir* had been written by another author and had already appeared in another journal.

Under the editorship of Philip Harwood, W. J. Loftie had joined the staff of the *Saturday Review* in 1874, and from that time, his wife, Martha Jane Loftie, also began to contribute articles. A survey of the *Saturday Review* between 1874 and 1879 has identified a number of articles written by Mrs Loftie, which were later collected and published in book form by Macmillan as *Forty-six Social Twitters* (1879). Mrs Loftie's preface stated rather apologetically:

> In republishing articles written at different times on kindred subjects

it is almost impossible that there should not be a certain amount of repetition. It is almost equally impossible to cut out paragraphs without re-writing articles. These essays therefore remain for the most part as they appeared in the *Saturday Review*, from which they have been reprinted with the kind permission of the Editor.[52]

Written between 1875 and 1876, five of the essays in *Social Twitters*, 'New Houses', 'Doing-Up One's House', 'The Spare Room', 'Living on Flats' and, 'Furnishing', discussed housing, interior decoration and furnishings. A close reading has suggested that the article on 'The Spare Room', published by the *Saturday Review* in April 1876, was reworked to form the final chapter of Lady Barker's *The Bedroom and Boudoir*. Witness the following paragraph written by Mrs Loftie:

> To busy people of moderate wealth the acknowledged possession of a spare room represents an income-tax of several shillings in the pound. It means to be forced to take in lodgers all year round who do not pay, but who expect as much attention as if they were in an American Hotel – to be obliged, not only to supply them with free quarters, but to amuse, advise, chaperon, perhaps even nurse and bury them.[53]

Two years later, in a chapter also called 'The Spare Room', Lady Barker issued a very similar warning to her readers:

> To a professional man, with a small income, the institution of a spare room may be regarded as an income tax of several shillings in the pound. It is even worse than that; it means being forced to take in a succession of lodgers who don't pay, who are generally amazingly inconsiderate and *exigeante*, and who expect to be amused and advised, chaperoned and married, and even nursed and buried.[54]

Clearly Mrs Loftie's earlier article had been recycled, without attribution, for use in Lady Barker's volume in the 'Art at Home' series. Significantly, a review of *The Bedroom and Boudoir* published *The Spectator* in April 1878, had noted a change in style (if not author) and commented:

> The chapter on the 'Spare Room' does not say much for Lady Barker's hospitality, though it strikes one that she has taken up her views on the subject more as an excuse for a little smart writing, than because they express her real opinion.[55]

An examination of Mrs Loftie's 'smart writing' published by the *Saturday Review* suggests that she was rarely reticent in expressing her opinions, and this is also apparent in her descriptions of the *Scribner's* illustrations that appeared in *The Dining Room*. Throughout this volume, particularly in the third chapter on 'Sideboards, Tables and Chairs', Mrs Loftie made constant references to the *Scribner's* images, and like Mrs Orrinsmith, renamed and adapted them as she saw fit. On several occasions, against the advice of Frederick Macmillan, Mrs Loftie even used the American illustrations as examples of bad taste.[56] Thus, having quoted at length from a recent article in 'one of the weekly papers'[57] (which was probably one of her own) on the design faults of fashionable knick-knacks, she described an image of an ornately carved table as 'An example of the sort of furniture designed on the same false principles as these horrible inventions'.[58] The illustration list renamed this cut as 'AN EXAMPLE TO BE AVOIDED'. In contrast, when this woodcut of a 'Table and Chair from Tyrol, Bavaria' appeared in the tenth of the original articles in *Scribner's Monthly*, it had been described in detail and judged by Cook to be 'very pretty'.[59]

Opportune though it may have been for Macmillan & Co., the use of these American illustrations was hugely problematic, prompting not just critical reviews in the professional press, but transatlantic anxieties over copyright. Indeed, there was a delay in the production of the electrotypes because of concerns that Macmillan & Co., would use the images in books offered for sale in America – as they had fully intended: in a letter to Lady Barker dated July 1877, Craik mentioned the possibility of American sales.[60] Scribner's sought assurances that Macmillan would not sell the plates to their American associates, Porter & Coates of Philadelphia, and in reply, Macmillan wrote:

> We of course understand that Mr Clarence Cook's pictures are copyright and that no books containing them can be sold in the US. We are sorry that you have delayed making the electrotypes on this ground and beg that you will get them finished and sent off with as little delay as possible.[61]

Consequently, Macmillan informed Porter & Coates that they would be unable to publish these three volumes in America.

It is unfortunate that the last three volumes of the Art at Home series have contained so much copyright matter as to render them useless for American publication. We hope however, you will find it possible to take plates of several volumes which are now in preparation.[62]

The 'Art at Home' series was an Anglo-American publishing venture that sought to exploit the tide of enthusiasm for house decoration on both sides of the Atlantic. However, using these books as evidence of the design and decoration of the late-Victorian lower-middle class domestic interior is fraught with difficulties. Conceived as an intervention and advocating 'inconspicuous consumption', the series promoted an upper-middle class view of how lower-middle class aspirants should decorate, furnish and behave in their homes. The discourses discernible in the texts combined with biographical research suggest that the authors, though perhaps loosely linked along class lines, were writing from completely different religious, economic, political, marital and occupational positions, which had significant ramifications for the advice they gave. Moreover, the history of its production reveals that certain volumes in the series were based on essays, articles and papers previously published in a range of magazines: add the complication of the American illustrations and it becomes impossible to use Macmillan's 'Art at Home' series as conventional historical evidence. Consequently, while it remains an important source for considering nineteenth-century concepts of taste, class and gender, it may be that the 'Art at Home' series offers more information about the expedient world of nineteenth-century publishing practices than it does about the Victorian interior.

Notes

1 *The House Beautiful* was reissued by Charles Scribner's Sons, New York in 1881. Like the Garland Press reprint of 'Art at Home' series, *The House Beautiful* and Eastlake's *Hints on Household Taste* have since been reprinted by Dover Editions and have both received renewed interest.

2 N. Pevsner, 'Art Furniture of the 1870s' in *The Architectural Review*, CXI, 1952 (reprinted in *Studies in Art, Architecture and Design*, vol. 2, London: Thames & Hudson, 1969); E. Aslin, *The Aesthetic Movement: Prelude to Art Nouveau* (London: Elek Books, 1969); M. Girouard, *Sweetness and Light: The 'Queen Anne Movement' 1860 –1900* (Yale University Press, 1977); P. Thornton, *Authentic Décor, The Domestic Interior, 1620 –1920* (Weidenfeld & Nicolson, 1984); A. Forty, *Objects of Desire: Design and Society 1750 –1980* (Thames &

Hudson, 1986); A. Briggs, *Victorian Things* (Penguin, 1988); J. Banham et al., *Victorian Interior Style* (Studio Editions, 1995); T. Logan, *The Victorian Parlour: A Cultural Study* (Cambridge University Press, 2001); H. Long, *Victorian Houses and their Details: The Role of Publications in their Building and Decoration* (Architectural Press, 2002); and, C. Gere and L. Hoskins, *The House Beautiful – Oscar Wilde and the Aesthetic Interior* (Lund Humphries/ Geffrye Museum, 2002).

3 M. Girouard, 1977; 1984, p. 211.

4 N. Humble, 'Introduction', in *Mrs Beeton's Book of Household Management* (Oxford World Classics, 2000; first published 1861), p. xvi.

5 British Library Manuscripts Collection: Macmillan & Co Ltd, publishers 1833–1969: Add. MSS 54786–56035, 61894–96; Reading University Library: Macmillan & Co Ltd, publishers 1875–1964: MS 1089.

6 BL: Add. MS 55075/122/124/126/128. W. J. Loftie to Macmillan, 11 March 1876.

7 BL: Add. MS 55075/118. W. J. Loftie to Macmillan, 29 February 1876.

8 BL: Add. MS 55075/122/124/126/128. W. J. Loftie to Macmillan, 11 March 1876.

9 Loftie suggested Stevenson, on the strength of an article on 'Our Dwelling Houses' published in *Good Words* in October 1873. Eventually, Macmillan published the two volumes of J. J. Stevenson's *House Architecture* separately in 1880, and although it was not issued as part of the 'Art at Home' series, Loftie was still involved with the production of this publication.

10 Ibid. Margaret Plues, was a writer and expert on wild flowers and grasses.

11 BL: Add. MS 55399/64. A. Macmillan to Rev. W. J. Loftie, 14 March 1876.

12 BL: Add. MS 55075/136. W. J. Loftie to Macmillan, 12 August 1876. James Davis Cooper (1823–1901) seems to have engraved most of the illustrations for the first four volumes. R. K. Engen, *Dictionary of Victorian Wood Engravers* (Cambridge: Chadwyck-Healey, 1985), p. 54, described Cooper as a 'Prominent London wood engraver and draughtsman on wood, who engraved after the major artists of his day'.

13 Harry Soane fl. 1840–95: According to R. K. Engen, 1985, p. 244, Soane was a London wood engraver, heraldic draughtsman and stationer, who worked at Green Street, Leicester Square WC.

14 *The Saturday Review*, 25 November, 1876, pp. 656–657. The wallpaper referred to appears to be Morris's 'Trellis'.

15 *Dictionary of National Biography*: Supplement January 1901–December 1911, OUP, 1958 reprint, pp. 474–475 'Loftie, William John (1839–1911)', p. 474.

16 Ibid., pp. 474–475.

17 M. M. Bevington, *The Saturday Review 1855–1868: Representative Educated Opinion in Victorian England* (Columbia University Press, 1941) has demonstrated that John Hullah and Andrew Lang both contributed articles to the journal, while W. H. Pollock later became its editor (1883–94).

18 'Art at Home', *The Manchester Examiner*, November 1876; *The Transactions of the National Association for the Promotion of Social Science* 1876, pp. 863–865, noted that Rhoda Garrett's paper was also published in *Macmillan's Magazine*.

19 BL: Add. MS 55401/71. A. Macmillan to Miss R. Garrett, 6 December 1876. Cliché in this sense means a metal casting of a stereotype or electrotype.

20 Reprinted in Rev. W. J. Loftie, 1876. See the 1879 edition for advertisements, p. 2.

21 BL: Add. MS 55075/118. W. J. Loftie to Macmillan, 29 February 1876.

22 *The Saturday Review*, 25 November, 1876, p. 657.

23 *The Furniture Gazette*, Saturday 9 December 1876, p. 349.

24 BL: Add. MS 55400/882. Macmillan & Co., to Messrs J. H Coates & Co., 27 November 1876.

25 *The American Architect and Building News*, 12 May, 1877, p. 149.

26 Ibid.

27 E. Ferry, 'Decorators may be compared to doctors: An analysis of Rhoda and Agnes Garrett's *Suggestions for House Decoration in Painting, Woodwork and Furniture* (1876)', *Journal of Design History*, vol. 16, no. 1, 2003, pp. 15–34.

28 BL: Add. MS 55075. W. J. Loftie to Macmillan, 2 August 1876.

29 Mrs M. E. Haweis, *The Art of Decoration* (London: Chatto & Windus, 1881), pp. 336–337.

30 C. M. Cook, 'Beds and Tables, Stools and Candlesticks – Some Chapters on House Furnishing', in *Scribner's Monthly*, vol. X, no. 12, June 1875, p. 169.

31 Gere and Hoskins, 2002, p. 81.

32 BL: Add. MS 55402/351. F. Macmillan to W. J. Loftie, 16 April 1877. One wonders what the Anglo-Irish Loftie made of Cook's abhorrent anti-Irish comments, where he blamed 'the Biddy tribe from the bogs of Ireland' for a long list of social ills. C. M. Cook, *The House Beautiful* (New York: Dover Publications and London: Constable and Co., 1995: first published 1877), p. 271.

33 BL: Add. MS 55402/372. F. Macmillan to C. M. Cook, 18 April 1877.

34 BL: Add. MS 55402/372. Macmillan & Co., to Messrs Scribner, Armstrong & Co., New York, 18 April 1877 and BL: Add. MS 55402/372. Macmillan

& Co., to Messrs Scribner, Armstrong & Co., New York, 4 June 1877. See S. Eliot, in E. James (ed.), *Macmillan: A Publishing Tradition* (Palgrave, 2002), p. 51 n. 28. 'One of the striking features of Macmillan production is its strong inclination to electrotype, as oppose to stereotype, when producing plates. The former is more expensive and technically trickier, but frequently gives finer results as well as producing more copies.'

35 BL: Add. MS 55402/392. A. Macmillan to Rev. W. J. Loftie, 20 April 1877.

36 BL: Add. MS 55402/954. G. L. Craik to Rev. W. J. Loftie, 27 June 1877; BL: Add. MS 55403/306. G. L. Craik to Rev. W. J. Loftie, 31 July 1877.

37 The book is dedicated to George Lillie Craik. See Mrs Orrinsmith, 'Dedication', *The Drawing Room* (Macmillan, 1877).

38 C. M. Cook, 1877; 1995, pp. 65–66.

39 Mrs Orrinsmith, 1877, p. 78.

40 Nonetheless, Thad Logan has recently used this extract from *The Drawing Room* to indicate the popularity of Japanese style screens made fashionable by the aesthetic movement. See T. Logan, 2001, p. 120.

41 Mrs Orrinsmith, 1877, p. 93.

42 BL: Add. MS. 55404/236. Macmillan & Co., to the editor of *Building News*, 19 November 1877.

43 *British Architect and Northern Engineer*, 3 July 1874.

44 E. W. Godwin 'In the Art at Home Series' in *The British Architect and Northern Engineer*, 8 February 1878, p. 64. Godwin also publicly chastised the Garretts for stealing his design for a side table that they illustrated in the frontispiece of *Suggestions for House Decoration*. See Letter to William Watt, 1 January 1877 and printed in *Art Furniture designed by Edward W. Godwin FSA and manufactured by William Watts, 21 Grafton Street London, with hints and suggestions on domestic furniture and decoration*, 1877, p. iii.

45 Lady M. A. Barker, *The Bedroom and Boudoir* (Macmillan, 1878), p. 64.

46 C. M. Cook, 1877; 1995, pp. 290–291.

47 Lady M. A. Barker, 1878, pp. 50–51.

48 Ibid., p. 81.

49 'Art at Home', *The Spectator*, 13 April 1878, p. 476.

50 Lady M. A. Barker, 1878, p. 89.

51 Ibid., p. 90.

52 Mrs M. J. Loftie, 'Preface', *Forty-six Social Twitters* (Macmillan & Co., 1879).

53 Mrs M. J. Loftie, 'The Spare Room', *The Saturday Review*, vol. XLI, 29 April 1876, pp. 545–546.

54 Lady M.A. Barker, 1878, pp. 115–116.

55 *The Spectator*, 13 April 1878, p. 476.

56 BL: Add. MS. 55404/387. F. Macmillan to W.J. Loftie, 3 December 1877.

57 Mrs M.J. Loftie, *The Dining Room* (Macmillan, 1878), p. 19.

58 Ibid.

59 C.M. Cook, 'Talk Here and There: Beds and Tables, Stools and Candlesticks, X' in *Scribner's Monthly*, p. 820; reprinted in *The House Beautiful*, 1877, p. 255. This illustration was copied from an engraving in M. Rodolphe Pfnor's *Ornamentation Usuelle*, 1866–1867.

60 BL: Add. MS 55403/301. G.L. Craik to Lady Barker, 30 July 1877.

61 BL: Add. MS 55403/22. Macmillan & Co., to Messrs Scribner, Armstrong & Co., 2 July 1877.

62 BL: Add. MS 55405/429. Macmillan & Co., to Messrs Porter & Coates, 9 March 1878.

8 ✧ *Design* magazine – a conversation, 22 September 2003

Gillian Naylor and Ken Garland

I n 1944 the British Board of Trade announced the founding of the Council of Industrial Design to 'promote by all practicable means the improvement of design products of British industry'.[1] Five years later, in 1949, the Council launched a powerful weapon in this cultural assault, the propagandist magazine *Design*. Targeted at professional designers, manufacturers, company buyers and managers, the publication's remit was to increase the market for well-designed products by exposing its readers to examples of 'good design'. The following conversation between two of the magazine's staff, Ken Garland, Art Director, and Gillian Naylor, writer, not only reveals the various freedoms and constraints of working within the British design establishment during the 1950s and 1960s, it also signals the beginnings of an increasingly self-conscious attitude towards the history of design in Britain.

Gillian Naylor: When I joined *Design* magazine in 1956 you were already on the staff, and I never thought to ask about your previous career. I know you trained as a graphic designer, but why did you decide in the first-place to become a graphic designer?

Ken Garland: I left secondary school at 16 to go to an art school – the West of England Academy of Art at Bristol where there was no such thing as Graphic Design. There was a course called Commercial Design and I wasn't quite sure what it was but I knew that I could pursue some sort of art and make a living out of it.

When I came to London after I'd done military service I tried to get into the Central School of Arts and Crafts without success. I went to the Sir John Cass College of Art and the course there was something called the National Diploma in Design and it included all sorts of things; it was a general art and design education. By my second year I realised it didn't suit my purpose and I extricated myself from there eventually.

GN: So what dates were these?

KG: 1952–3. I managed to get to the Central School, which was running a course in what they had just begun to call Graphic Design – formerly it had been called Book Production and then they got the 'graphic design notion', as it were. The course was headed by a very far-seeing head of department called Jesse Collins and some excellent tutors. In particular he employed Anthony Froshaug and Herbert Spencer.

GN: The Central had a long tradition of teaching lettering and graphic art. So you'd gone to the Mecca as it were.

KG: Yes, I thought it was the right place, and it was. The tutors' methods of teaching were very distinctive and complementary. Froshaug had an affirmative, almost bullying style of teaching. He would give us projects but he was more interested in the process and in stimulating debate than in reaching a solution. Herbert Spencer was much more laid back and quiet so they made an interesting contrast. Spencer had published a book called *Design In Business Printing* in 1952, which became really quite a significant contribution to our field.[2]

GN: Presumably there were very few people writing about graphics at that time?

KG: Do you know, it wasn't until I went to an evening class in photography run by a man named Nigel Henderson that I heard about the Bauhaus![3] Would you believe that they could conduct a course in graphic design without mentioning László Moholy-Nagy or Walter Gropius or Herbert Bayer? It was quite extraordinary. Nonetheless, I did begin to latch onto them during my time at Central.

GN: Was the programme influenced by Swiss graphics?

KG: Yes. Anthony Froshaug was constantly referring to Swiss graphics and they were certainly seen as a kind of a model, a model which I came to treat with suspicion later on; except I was very interested in Jan Tschichold (who, of course, was German not Swiss) and was the great pioneer in asymmetric typography, as he called it. He produced a book called *Typographische Gestaltung* (Asymmetric Typography).[4] First published in 1935, the book was a kind of transition. He was already moving away from the absolutism of early asymmetric typography which had been taken up so enthusiastically by the Swiss. And he was having fierce debates and rows with Max Bill.[5] Herbert Spencer knew quite a bit about him, Froshaug knew more and he loaned me his copy of *Typographische Gestaltung* and related great chunks of it to me.

GN: You must have been a prize student?

KG: I was one of about half-a-dozen students in my year who were spoken to. The rest he had little time for.

GN: I'll try to fill in some of my background. I came from Yorkshire and studied French at Somerville College, Oxford. I came to London where initially I worked with a publisher and then went for the job advertised on *Design* magazine. I wanted some sort of work where I was writing. I didn't want to pursue the French specialisation. I didn't want to translate or teach French. A graduate employment officer usually advised girls to apply for the Civil Service or to do a secretarial course. I wanted to write and so I was applying for all sorts of jobs which would allow me to do that.

I knew about The Design Centre but I hadn't given it any major study so I did what I thought was my homework: I looked at the magazine and looked at the architectural and interior design press and the *Architectural Review* and I got an interview. I can't remember what happened at the first interview but I was short-listed for the second one along with six others. I was horrified because I had to do an intelligence test and was really stymied when I had to do some sums ... long division in pounds, shillings and pence. Then I was given news items to summarise (press releases – the job was for a news editor). Finally I went to see Michael Farr, the editor of *Design*, in his office; he had illustrations of various objects on the wall and I had to say which ones were good design – which wasn't terribly difficult! Then he asked me what I'd been reading and I'd read some of Gordon Cullen's writing in the *Architectural Review*. And then he asked whether I had seen any exhibitions of good design other than those in The Design Centre. Fortunately I'd recently been to the V&A to see an exhibition of silverware, and in the corridor leading to the restaurant there was a wonderful display of Finnish fabrics. They were in the most glorious colours that all melted into each other and I said I'd like to buy some to furnish the bedsit where I was living. I think that must have got me some brownie points – anyway, I got the job and joined the staff.

What struck me when I first arrived at *Design* magazine were my colleagues. I had never before worked with people who were so committed to their work and who had a vision and wanted to see this vision realised. At Oxford, being in a woman's college, we did talk about our work, of course, but in general there was a sense, especially for men, that it wasn't really done to talk 'shop'. So I was fascinated by the climate at *Design* magazine and the debates about why design mattered.

It took me some time but I began to realise that this commitment to 'good design' was value-laden. These ideas and attitudes had a history and that's when I became interested in the history of design. I started to try to find out who Gropius was, for instance. I think the Bauhaus was mentioned in my first week. I had to write a news item about the Hochschule für Gestaltung at Ulm [The design school at Ulm was founded in 1951 and originally aimed to follow Bauhaus principles]. William Morris was also important. I remember once in an editorial, C. R. Ashbee was spelt Ashby and Gordon Russell, then Director of the CoID pointed this out and said, 'These are the people this institution is founded upon and you must at the very least get their names right in the magazine!'

KG: I remember this sense of commitment was communicated to me from the very first interview I had with Michael Farr for the job at *Design* magazine. Farr had inherited quite a lot of the Arts and

Crafts ideas. He'd been a student of Pevsner and, of course, his boss at the Council of Industrial Design was Gordon Russell – a true inheritor of Arts and Crafts notions but he also had his own technological notion about design. And his first question to me in my interview was, 'Do you know what cybernetics are?' I thought, hmm … it's not an 'are' it's an 'is'. But I gave him a rough definition of it and he said, 'Well, you're the first graphic designer who's attempted any definition of cybernetics,' which helped me no end. I soon realised that he had a sort of double commitment. One was to the sensible English design tradition and the other was to his interest in technology relating to ergonomic factors.

GN: With Michael you had to rationalise good design. You had to explain exactly what it was.

KG: Yes. It was intensely irritating. I'd say, 'Well I just think such and such is good design,' and he'd say, 'Why?' It was a marvellous discipline for me. It often seemed irrelevant but essentially this philosophy has stayed with me ever since. Meanwhile, ergonomics has come and gone and human factors have been first welcomed and then put aside. I remember industrial designers saying, 'Yes, let's give ergonomics a bit of a go for a year or two,' and that was their response – and there we all were thinking it was the future!

GN: I wasn't necessarily thinking ergonomics was the future. Perhaps it's something to do with gender … but describing 'good design' at that time was very difficult. I used to write the captions for the 'Design Index' articles. This featured objects which had been selected by the CoID'S design panel on grounds of 'good design'. I wrote the captions. But the panel wouldn't let us know how they had reached their decisions. There was not much space … about three or four lines. I could describe materials and working processes, but I could not sum up style in a few words.

KG: There was a dichotomy going on because some of the things on the Index had been accepted on grounds of taste. Taste wasn't very important to Michael (partly because he didn't have much himself!). He was always looking for functional reasons why something was good design and sometimes those reasons just didn't exist. Michael got into big rows with Gordon Russell and Russell's deputy, Paul Reilly, and other people who thought that *Design* magazine was being very uppity about certain objects.

GN: That's right, because the Trustees and Members of the Council were often manufacturers and if you analysed one of their objects and found it didn't work there could be trouble. I'm not sure when the magazine introduced the 'Design Analysis' articles by Bruce Archer.[6] They became quite controversial because they took a critical stance. There was a huge furore over the Morphy Richards toaster for instance which had been accepted for 'Design Index'. [The toaster sometimes caught fire when it was used.]

KG: *Design* magazine was meant to be an independent organ. Of course, it wasn't. It was financed by, controlled by and responsible to the Council of Industrial Design; a very, very interesting dichotomy – an unending source of amusement and excitement. I remember one year at the Design Centre Awards which grew out of the Design Index (and included the Duke of Edinburgh's Awards for Elegant Design) [we're all snorting!]). One of the awards that year was for a Robin Day day-bed produced by Hille Furniture. The awards were featured by Cliff Michelmore on the 'Tonight' TV programme. Michelmore was a mischievous personality and he was leaning on the back of this chair and saying, 'Well, what does this do?' and Robin Day said, 'Well, it turns into a double bed.' 'Do you mean like this?' said Michelmore and he leant back and, of course, the bed collapsed backwards with him and Robin Day in it. Day was covered in confusion and we thought this was most hilarious because it demonstrated that the bed wasn't really such a good design. The incident exemplified the kind of concerns that *Design* magazine was interested in.

GN: I think it's important to point out that we were always being briefed that *Design* wasn't a 'consumer magazine'. We weren't sold on the railway stations, or in bookshops etc. Occasionally you could buy it at Smith's stationers, but it was not widely on sale to the general public. Our circulation was primarily among the manufacturing industry – it was aimed at industry and designers.

KG: I imagine the industrialists reading it with some malicious glee when they saw some sniping at their competitors and then in the following issue finding something written against them. We were in hot water a lot of the time.

GN: Yes, we tried various ways of being subversive. We would show photographs of the Design Index panel and the Duke of Edinburgh thinking about 'What is Good Design?' and we always chose the worst photos. I remember Paul Reilly looking at a picture of the Duke of Edinburgh and saying, 'Couldn't you come up with anything better?' and Ken, you had some very persuasive arguments as to how difficult he was to photograph. I'm sure a lot of magazines operate like that, and certainly newspapers do.

KG: The magazine was funded partly by its sales and partly by a grant so it didn't actually have to break even. Later, it was increasingly funded by advertising which burgeoned during your, and my time, at the magazine. The size of *Design* itself went from 48 pages to around 100 and a great deal of that was advertising.

GN: Yes I was surprised when looking through some back copies at how much there was. You supervised the placing of the advertisements didn't you?

KG: Yes. I was responsible for placing the ads and I did this on grounds of merit of their design, which didn't suit a lot of the advertisers! They would complain that they never got the back cover or the inside back cover and I'd give them the reasons why they didn't get better placing and try to encourage them to improve their designs. It very rarely worked, I'm afraid.

There was another employee who was responsible for advertising – he was the Finance Director of the CoID, Arthur Sudbery. It was a very different situation from my previous incarnation on a trade magazine whereby the Advertising Director was basically the boss of the magazine and would tell us all what to feature. Sudbery didn't want advertisers running the magazine and neither did Michael Farr. How we managed to maintain relations with our advertisers by treating them in such a cavalier fashion I don't know. However, we were considered to be the golden boys and girls by the

CoID because we were pulling in revenue for them, and although I don't know for certain, I believe that the magazine ended up paying for itself.

GN: Let's get back to the 1950s and 1960s. Tell me about what you were reading at the time.

KG: Five works that were influential to me were: *Vision in Motion* by Moholy-Nagy, *The Language of Vision* by Gyorgy Kepes, *An Essay on Typography* by Eric Gill, *Typographische Gestaltung* by Jan Tschichold, and *Design in Business Printing* by Herbert Spencer (as previously mentioned).[7] These works were all very important to me during the time that I was working on *Design* magazine. While I was there a book emerged called *The New Graphic Art* written by Karl Gerstner and Markus Kutter (Swiss designers).[8] There also emerged a magazine called *neue graphik* which was produced by four Zurich based graphic designers and to me it was anathema. It was bad, bad, bad and yet my fellow designers thought it was revelatory. None of them could read the text and see what drivel it was. I mention that because it shows my separation from, and differences with, the more absolutist notions of graphic design. It was one of the reasons why *Design* magazine was the way it was and not more 'Swiss'.

This leads on to the notion of the difference between things that are pragmatic and things that are more idealistic. Bruce Archer started a series in the magazines which attempted to show the tensions between the two viewpoints relating to design. I was always interested in exploring the pragmatic side of design, unlike some of my fellow designers who didn't always care about legibility or readability or anything like that (a view fostered by people like Max Bill, Carlo Vivarelli, and Hans Neuberg, some of whom I met when I went to Switzerland in the 1960s – a most interesting encounter!)

GN: You changed the layout of *Design* I believe? Can you describe your approach to the magazine's visual appearance?

KG: Yes I changed the layout in 1956. It had some strange features – the title style was a slab serif and it also had the two-storey g which

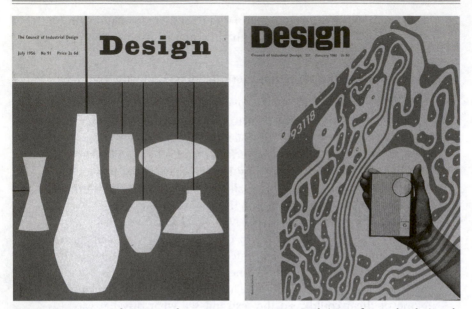

8.1 *Design*, no. 91, July 1956 and no. 157, January 1962. Both issues featured redesigned mastheads by Ken Garland.

was anathema to the Swiss. I continued that in the new logo which came out in 1962 and was a sans serif. 'Why are you persisting with the two-storey g?' said one of my fellow designers. I said, 'Well, it's a British g – why the hell not?' I felt it was a more friendly, less intimidating design. (Incidentally, that masthead has remained the same for the last 30 years. Occasionally people would ask, 'Do you think should it be redesigned?' and I'd say, 'Well, of course, it should' – just for the hell of it if nothing else! How are graphic designers going to have any fun if you won't let them redesign things?)

Furthermore, I didn't insist on having a consistent starting-point, or chapter-drop for text – something that was very common at the time. I varied it from feature to feature. Having a mannerism that ran through the magazine seemed pointless to me – I wanted to suit the layout to the subject-matter. It seemed that certain subjects demanded certain approaches. Design to the Swiss was about standardisation, having a certain grid and then a pattern and whatever the subject matter they would approach it the same way. I totally opposed this kind of conformity.

GN: There was also the *Penrose Annual* which we've not mentioned ...?

KG: I wrote an article in the *Penrose Annual* in 1960 called 'Structure and Substance'. In my piece I juxtaposed American and Swiss graphic design without taking a firm stand on either. There was merit on both styles of design but I suggested that we could probably find a middle way and use the best elements of both of them. In terms of US graphic design I was looking at the work of Saul Bass and some British work which I thought had the spontaneity of the US work as well as the more disciplined forms of the Swiss.

GN: Can you describe the practicalities of working on *Design*? Did you have to present everything you planned to feature to Michael Farr for instance?

KG: On the whole, it was a case of me presenting proposals to Michael Farr and him saying yes, no or maybe and on the whole it was, yes. Some people found him a real tyrant but to me he was always sympathetic and we got on well. We did have occasional disputes but nothing like the kind I heard about between other editors and art editors.

GN: My experience as a contributing journalist was that Ken was the one who told you how many words you had to write! We used to have these work-in-progress meetings early in the week where we would discuss how we were getting on with the magazine that was due to come out – check that the authors had been briefed, find the photographers, etc., that kind of thing. And then we would also have meetings where we would look ahead and discuss the kind of articles that we should be having. While I was there it was getting more and more focused on ergonomics and moving away from the domestic environment.

In addition, the Council of Industrial Design used to feed us material which they wanted us to feature in the magazine. The Council had two sections; it had the Industrial Section where there was an officer in charge of various industries and the Information Division which would also feed us material and ideas for articles that we should run, on issues like the disabled and education, etc. Instead of pressure from advertisers this was where our pressure was coming from and we obviously had to be very tactful about the objects we included.

For instance, Dan Johnson was the Industrial Officer for textiles and he was a lovely man but he always thought in terms of traditional chintz and he would bring us fabrics which we did not want to include in *Design* magazine.

Speaking of which, let's consider this feature where you're trying to find ways of photographing furnishing fabrics in a very unconventional way …

KG: I'd like to firstly raise a practical matter about this spread which contains a mixture of black-and-white and colour photographs.

8.2 The fleeting figure is used as a prop in Ken Garland's photo shoot from *Design*, no. 153, September 1961.

This was not because I thought it would create an interesting effect or anything, but because certain of the manufacturers were not prepared to pay the additional supplement in order to have their products shown in colour. This was the most god-awful nuisance particularly where textiles were concerned, which usually tend to rely on colour. Even though all the manufacturers featured would share the cost of the colour printing between them, some of the small companies still didn't think they could afford to pay the difference between colour and black-and-white so you were faced with a real problem.

Anyway, in this shoot I used a prop – a fleeting figure. It actually developed from a previous series of photographs of floor coverings which got a lot of attention [spread showing floor coverings with objects on them].[9] I actually got asked to do some commercial work following on from that which I turned down. Harriet Crowder, one of the staff photographers, and I worked in close partnership for that series but I was actually the one who came up with all the props. I just say that because I was always interested in setting up and playing around with unusual ways of showing the products.

GN: The textiles were from the CoID's selected objects of 'good design', this Design Index, a section of the design council's premises, was mainly made up of the manufacturers 'hand-out' photographs.[10] Were you also given these to use?

KG: Yes, but gradually I moved to using fewer and fewer of these handouts. There were two staff photographers, Alfred Lammer and Harriet Crowder, and we also used the work of a freelance photographer called John Garner who was particularly skilled at working with people. The manufacturers' commercial photographs would usually feature isolated objects but I wanted to show people interacting with things. Originally, there weren't any people in *Design* magazine except in the news features. John loved working with people and so from 1959 I employed him regularly.

GN: Yes, I remember John. He did a lot of photographs for us and I went out on several assignments with him. He worked by

John Garner

LIVING ROOM

Focus on what in the living room ? Do you sit and stare at blazing logs, flames leaping high, a symbol of another time and place ? Do you pull up the chairs, tight-circled, loose covers to the floor to keep off draughts ; or make believe with artificial flames that give electric warmth ? These are not for honest men today. Focus rather on a friend's face across the coffee table, or on the view from the window, or on television. Break up the circle, re-arrange the chairs (space to clean under and light to move). Plan the living room to serve a changing need. Sink back on rubber webbing or lateral springs. Turn the knob that brings your favourite programme into the room, on to the magic lantern of a modern age. Consider it a problem for design. Why disguise it in a more familiar shape ? Why not make it look like ∴ ... well, for example, a television set ? (Make a note to think more about this.) The room divider divides – but not quite – houses books, the radio, glass that sparkles, perhaps too much. Behind, trees spread across printed paper on the wall. Light glides along a table, from near the floor, above the chair – it is needed there to read. Or records (largest luxury industry) turn in stereophonic bliss. So regroup, replan, change round to focus on something new. Allow freedom to change and space to move – to live in comfort.

8.3 Article from *Design*, no. 121, January 1959, text by Sir Gordon Russell, photography by John Garner.

producing hundreds of contact prints, and then you both picked out the images you preferred.

KG: As far as I know Design Index later started using photographs that we'd taken.

GN: Michael Farr got very worked up about carpets and fabrics generally because he needed a rationale for deciding what was good design. One set of fabrics he selected for the magazine were by Tibor Reich. Reich had taken photographs of natural forms ... leaves, flowers and especially bark, and he blew up the photos to create abstractions and based the design of his fabrics on these. This was 'truth to nature'.

Michael believed that many carpet and rug manufacturers were trying to turn abstract art into industrial design and getting it wrong.

KG: Another photographer I enjoyed working with was Dennis Hooker, Alfred Lammer's predecessor. He was very amenable and appreciative and very keen to please me so obviously we got on well!

GN: Did you feel you were moving away from a genre of object photography, if indeed there was a distinct genre? What were the models for object photography and what were the techniques of your colleagues on the magazine?

KG: Well, the photographers were originally concerned with getting the lighting right and the shadows right so that you could see every detail. I was more interested in creating a dramatic effect, though not to the exclusion of detail. They were sold on the three-quarter view and I was very bored with the three-quarter view – I wanted to see something from the side or from above. However, I think in quality terms we were all very concerned with making things as good as they possibly could be, whereas a lot of commercial photographers would just want to knock things off quickly.

GN: I'm sure your work did have an impact on design photography in general. I remember going with Fred Lammer to photograph Coventry cathedral when it was opened. We had to do the photography before the cathedral was open to the public. In spite of the pressure on time his concentration was impressive. He would measure the light, check the angles, etc., before he got his camera out. This could take him half an hour … but his photographs were beautiful.

KG: Gillian – when you accompanied the photographer were you responsible for doing the research for the article as well?

GN: No, not always. Michael or I would brief the author and then sometimes I would go around with them to choose things to illustrate. I remember, for instance, choosing rugs in Kidderminster, going around wallpaper factories, carpet and ceramic factories and seeing how things were made. I was determined (and this is probably very gender-orientated) to stay with the material that I was interested in and I was not interested, for instance, in ergonomics. I mean, I didn't see ergonomics as the be-all and end-all, as Michael did. So I concentrated on domestic design, interiors, graphic design, design education, etc. I remember in my first week I was sent to interview Robin Darwin [the Rector of the Royal College of Art]; he was a difficult man and I reckon it was because no one else on the staff had the patience to interview him. I interviewed Richard Beeching (who was made Chairman of the British Transport Commission in 1961) when a design manual was being planned for British Rail. I did a lot of work on house styles, motorway signs, etc., which I could use when I started teaching. That was the sort of work that I was doing.

We had several editorial staff. John Blake was the Deputy Editor and he had a different approach to Michael. He trained as a painter at the Royal College of Art and had edited *Ark* magazine and he was a perfect back-up to Michael. He was patient and equally dedicated to good design. He got some negative press from the Independent Group who believed he'd become too conventional in the transition from the RCA to the CoID, but John stuck to his convictions. How did you react to those ideas of a contemporary avant-garde, Ken? You were a modern designer, an avant-garde designer, and you were based within an institution which could have been perceived as representing the establishment. Was it ever a problem?

KG: No, because we felt we were engaging not only in a battle with industrial manufacturers but also with the CoID itself. For example, while we were there the Consumer's Association was born and they started to do real object-testing of a kind which had not been done before. They began to look at things very critically – including things that had been approved of for design awards and that we had featured but in fact had been suspicious of – a set of saucepans for instance – that were absolutely destroyed by the Consumer's Association. Michael was gleeful about this but Paul Reilly was quite upset because the CoID was made to look foolish. Later in 'Design Analysis' we were able to approach something of the critical stance of the Consumer's Association.

Similarly if you asked Paul Reilly whether he saw himself as a pillar of the establishment he would vehemently deny it – he had a respectable past as a left-wing journalist! He said to me once in a confidential interview, 'You know Ken, I like a man with fire in his belly.'

GN: Gordon Russell was very supportive and helpful to me when I was on *Design* magazine. It was when I was there that I started to research and write books on the Arts and Crafts movement and the Bauhaus.

KG: I must tell you a story about Gordon Russell. In 1957, early on in my time at *Design* magazine I was asked to appear on the TV show 'Panorama'. I was asked to discuss the literature which was used to promote our exports internationally. I waved a lot of things about in front of the cameras saying how crummy they all were and caused quite a lot of fuss. Gordon Russell asked me to go and see him and said, 'Look I'm in a bit of trouble because a lot of my staff are rather upset with what you've been saying but listen here. Could you tell me, there's one thing that puzzles me, what is "crummy"?' So I tried to explain what it meant, with difficulty, and he said, 'Oh good good, perhaps I'll use it occasionally. How do you spell it? Crumby or crummie?' I said you can spell it whichever way you prefer.

Can I mention this article from March 1960 where I wrote about good magazine design and things I admired at the time? [Figure 8.4] On the whole there weren't many design magazines I found interesting although there were two American magazines, one called *Interiors* and one called *Industrial Design* and if I had a model it would be these magazines. They were both published by Whitney publications and we used to receive these publications with great eagerness every month. I wrote to the art editors and the editors and included them in my article. The article used some European as well as American magazines. The other one was on British design only and I felt I had less to choose from. Anyway, I did choose a couple, including *Queen* magazine, which I thought used photographs in a really exciting way.

I compared magazine design problems with the problems of

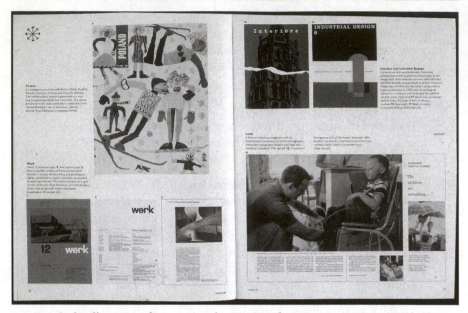

8.4 Ken Garland's survey of international magazines from *Design*, no. 135, March 1960.

making a film because I felt they had something in common. The way I saw it was that the process of turning a magazine's pages had something to do with the time lapses involved in film. This was quite a radical thought, in a way, although I did know that Willy Fleckhaus, the editor of *Twen*, one of the magazines from Germany that I featured in the international survey, was very interested in the cinematic properties of magazines. That magazine subsequently declined in quality because Fleckhaus who had been the art editor was later made the editor. I always think this to be a great mistake because you lose the tension and dialectic between the editor and the art editor. It's a very interesting relationship – I used to enjoy the discussions with Michael Farr – I thought we both came out rather better from the debate.

A guy that I praised in the British survey, Mark Boxer, became a friend shortly after my features had been published, and said how about some of us art editors getting together. From that conversation we met up with other art editors – Tom Wolsey from *Town* magazine, Sidney King and Derek Cousins from *Fusion* magazine and Barry Trengove, art editor of the new magazine *Honey*, and we informally became the art directors' lunch club. Tony Armstrong-Jones had by that time joined the CoID's panel at the suggestion of his friend, Mark Boxer, I took him along to one of the lunches. He was very impressed with them and enjoyed it a lot.

GN: Was there any connection between the lunch club and the organisation, D&AD [Design and Art Direction]?

KG: Yes, some of the people involved in that were the founder members of the D&AD it's true …

GN: I enjoyed working with Bruce Archer. He believed in a scientific and objective approach to design, and he wrote the Design Analysis articles which I was editing at the time and finding photographs for. I certainly enjoyed following his ideas and seeing how they built up into the criticisms of particular objects. In 1960 I went with the Design and Industries Association and with Michael Farr on a visit to Germany which was a revelation – not only for the design experience, but because I hadn't been abroad much before then. It was very difficult to get abroad then in the late 50s and early 60s, and of course *Design* magazine had to be careful about how it spent its money.

We went to a trade fair whilst we were there; we met Dieter Rams; we went to Munich and to Frankfurt. I peeled off with Mary Shand and we went to the Hochschule für Gestaltung at Ulm to see the work there. I was given contacts by Bruce [Archer] who had taught there. We stayed a couple of days, talking to the staff and students. It was very interesting because Tomas Maldonado was there then, developing his new policies.

It was during this time that I first started going to the Institute of Contemporary Arts. I had a lot to catch up on as far as painting and contemporary art (as well as design) was concerned. I had been interested in art and art history when I was at Oxford, but now I had London. So I went to a lot of exhibitions. I really enjoyed the debates and liveliness at the ICA. It also provided a counterblast to the ideas we were putting forward on the magazine. I did not have the tough-mindedness to say, 'There is one true way to design and to approach design.' I think that is one of the reasons that I became so interested in design's history – where these ideas were coming from and why.

        We also had an 'Overseas Review' section which I think John Blake edited but from time to time I edited it – these were articles sent in by the overseas correspondents. In Finland we had Olof Gummerus, in Germany we had Heinrich König – an ancient man with a club foot who came in with this fire of enthusiasm for the German Werkbund and what the Werkbund had done; he was working for the 'Rat für Formgebung' which was intended to carry on Werkbund ideals. Of course I didn't know anything about the Werkbund then but I began to become really interested in these organisations. Italian design (for instance, the work of Olivetti) was also featured and Letitia Ponti, the daughter of Gio Ponti also used to come in – she was very glamorous. She was introducing her father's furniture to the London department store, Liberty, and she said, 'I have come to London to make an exhibition of Father.' I went off with her and saw her father's chairs at Liberty which were fascinating because they seemed to be more within the English Arts and Crafts tradition than our own furniture at the time although I'm not sure I was rationalising it at the time. I remember talking to designers at Habitat from the period as well, not just Terence Conran, but all the various designers who were working for him, and to the buyers for Heals.

KG: *Design* magazine's international links were very strong. In addition to the Overseas Review we would insert material about foreign designers and producers into the magazine – which was quite contentious for, after all, we were supposed to be a magazine promoting British interests.

GN: I remember the great Wedgwood fracas. Michael was urging Wedgwood to produce modern British design, and Arthur Bryant, the head of the company at the time wrote to us explaining that the firm's strength was to produce traditional designs which were already extremely successful in the overseas markets. This was an obvious problem, but the CoID urged them to produce modern as well as traditional.

GN: Anthony Froshaug came to contribute to the magazine after you'd left. I would use his writing, Bruce Archer's writing and Reyner Banham (a subversive voice from the ICA who was writing on film, etc., in *The Spectator, New Society* and *The Listener*) when I was beginning to teach. I was also trying in my own way to pick up the histories of various industries – Alec Davies's book on packaging, for example, I found very helpful.

But why did you decide to leave *Design* magazine, Ken?

KG: I was having more fun than I'd ever had on *Design* magazine – I was given more initiative and had more responsibility than I'd experienced before, I was writing as well as designing, so it was extremely stimulating. I had to leave because my freelance work was also taking off at that time and I thought I really had to make a choice between that and between continuing at the magazine. I decided to leave whilst I was still very much enjoying it.

GN: I decided to leave in 1962 because I wanted to write about the Arts and Crafts movement and the Bauhaus. It is difficult to believe, but very little had been published about either when I began the research. I also wrote freelance for various magazines, and supplemented my income by teaching at Brighton and Kingston. And so, without realising it, I began my career as a design historian, a subject that was soon to be reinforced by the demands of the art colleges, and survives today; 'good design' having become part of history.

Notes

1 See C. and P. Fiell, *Industrial Design A–Z* (Köln, London: Taschen, 2000), p. 177.

2 H. Spencer, *Design in Business Printing* (London: Sylvan Press, 1952).

3 For a comprehensive survey of the influential photographer's work see V. Walsh, *Nigel Henderson: Parallel of Life and Art* (London: Thames & Hudson, 2001).

4 Jan Tschichold, *Typographische Gestaltung,* trans. R. Maclean (London: Faber, 1967).

5 Swiss-born German artist, designer, and architect, Max Bill, a product of the Bauhaus, went on to found the Hochschule für Gestaltung at Ulm. He remained an advocate of the new typography in the 1950s, whereas Tschichold revised his views in light of events under National Socialism, subscribing to a more moderate traditionalism.

6 The first 'Design Analysis' feature appeared in February 1957 written by J. Beresford-Evans. With thanks to Catherine Moriarty, Curator of the Design Council Archive, Brighton University, for her help in researching this point.

7 L. Moholy-Nagy, *Vision in Motion* (Chicago: Paul Theobold, 1947); G. Kepes, *The Language of Vision* (Chicago: Paul Theobold, 1944); E. Gill, *An Essay on Typography* (London: Sheed and Ward, 1931); J. Tschichold, *Typographische Gestaltung* (London: Faber, 1935); and H. Spencer, *Design in Business Printing* (London: Sylvan Press, 1952).

8 K. Gerstner and M. Kutter, *The New Graphic Art* (London: Alec Tiranti, 1959).

9 See *Design,* Issue 143, November 1960, 42–57.

10 C. Moriarty's article: 'A Backroom Service? The Photographic Library of the Council of Industrial Design, 1945–1965' is a fascinating discussion of the imagery used by the CoID to promote examples of 'good design', *Journal of Design History,* vol. 13, no. 1 (2000), 39–57.

9 ✧ *Crafts* for crafts' sake, 1973–88

Linda Sandino

IN March 1973 the Crafts Advisory Committee (CAC), launched its new magazine at the opening of *The Craftsman's Art* exhibition at the Victoria & Albert Museum.[1] The aim was to promote the work of the 'artist-craftsman'. The Royal Charter described the remit of the Crafts Council as follows:

> to advance and encourage the creation and conservation of works of fine craftsmanship and to foster, promote and increase the interest of the public in the works of craftsmen and the accessibility of those works to the public in England and Wales.[2]

Along with other gatekeeping initiatives such as the Index of selected makers, the exhibition programme, a collection, and the awarding of grants, the magazine became a key disseminator for the new crafts. However, the title, *Crafts*, and the magazine's contents came to represent the identity crisis of the handmade object in an emerging post-industrial world where, conventionally, craft had meant the deployment of traditional skills in the service of functional objectives.[3]

The sociologist Pierre Bourdieu noted how 'the fate of groups is bound up with the words that designate them' and the CAC is a case in point.[4] It became an active force in 'rebranding' craft in late twentieth-century Britain. The first issue featured the work of silversmith Michael Rowe, who epitomised the 'remarkable renaissance' that had taken place in craft activity.[5] His work was described as 'beyond the accepted confines of craft and into the realms of sculpture, architecture and even landscape'.[6] The choice of Rowe predicted some

of the debates that would take place in the magazine in the issues to
follow.

The period under scrutiny in this essay, and the context within which
the new crafts circulated, are intrinsically linked to the rise of an increasingly consumer orientated and aestheticised lifestyle. As noted by the
sociologist Mike Featherstone:

> [The] dual focus on a life of aesthetic consumption and the need to form
> life into an aesthetically pleasing whole on the part of artistic and intel-
> lectual countercultures, should be related to the development of mass
> consumption in general and the pursuit of new tastes and sensations
> and the construction of distinctive lifestyles which has become central
> to consumer culture.[7]

Furthermore, *Crafts* could be seen as one of the key producers of symbolic
capital as theorised by Bourdieu:

> accumulation [which] consists in making a name for oneself, a known
> recognised name, a capital of consecration implying a power to con-
> secrate objects (with a trademark of signature) or persons (through
> publication, exhibitions etc.) and therefore to give value.[8]

The magazine's role, therefore, was to be both the discoverer and creator
of the new craft producers by including and discussing their work in its
pages, by promoting appropriate galleries, exhibitions and events. The
economic promotion of the work was muted since the primary concern
of the publication was to act as a gallery without walls.

The covers of *Crafts* magazine

Appearing once every two months, *Crafts* was hampered as a newsstand publication and was initially sold primarily through subscriptions.
Consequently, the obliqueness of the early covers could be seen as
reflecting the ambivalence surrounding its readership and journalistic
purpose. Issues with traditional images of craft sold more copies than
those featuring obscure, indecipherable but, nevertheless, decorative
details.[9] Covers were chosen initially by the editors, with creative input
from their art directors. The first two editors, Marigold Coleman and
Martina Margetts were both journalists. Coleman had a background in

educational publishing; Margetts's experience included two and half years at *Harper's Bazaar*, and freelance writing for art journals.

John Hawkins, first art director of the magazine established the distinctive elegant simplicity of the magazine. Andrew Barron, who worked with both editors, followed the pristine quality of Hawkins's approach in which the new craft was mostly represented by the stylistic elegant detail.

Accessible images were still a problem in the early 1980s. Art Director, Bruce Brown (nos 41/1981 to 68/1984) made a distinction between a 'cover cover' and an editorial cover such as the Memphis glass vase on no. 59 (1982), an object of dispute, viewed by the Crafts Council as neither 'craft' nor English.[10]

> It is a picture that would be good against an editorial inside with a narrative but it does not say enough standing on its own. Provoking and saying, 'What is all this about?' It is not enough to say, 'People have got to read it,' because they will not. There has to be something on the cover that says, 'There's an answer to this funny thing you're looking at.'

The sometimes conflicting claims of editorial and art direction seem to have become more vexed from the early 1980s onwards. This was the result of the growing, new, articulate craft constituency, as well as the intellectual ambitions for the magazine of its editor, Martina Margetts.

If Roland Barthes construed fashion as a 'system of signs', craft was similarly beset by shifting signifiers and signifieds. Furthermore, the covers veered between oblique and populist in a manner that corresponds to Barthes' observations on fashion magazines.[11]

Covers from the 1970s represented the paradox of the magazine's need to maintain its conventional audience while cultivating the new image of craft-that-is-not-craft. The stronger rhetoric of the late 1980s was not the result of the success of the transformation. It was rather a shift from the elitist autonomy of the new art/craft object to an acknowledgement of the need to appeal to a wider audience; to become, in the words of another former art director, David King (nos 69–91), 'something like entertainment'.[12]

Crafting a publication

The CAC's brief to Marigold Coleman was to create a specialist magazine that, nevertheless, needed to maintain as broad a constituency as possible; the publication had to present the repositioning of the crafts while maintaining traditional notions of value and quality implicit in the ideology of the practice.

Initially the printing was by letterpress at Balding & Mansell using handmade blocks etched with acid but the skills required to continue with this craft method gave way in 1977 (no. 29) to lithography, resulting in a lighter print tone. This shift in production methods could be seen to symbolically mark the beginning of the attempts to integrate *Crafts* into the mainstream of magazine publishing. In 1981 (no. 52), Bruce Brown (who had seized the opportunity to work on a magazine that could vie with European models) changed to using non-glossy paper.[13] He subsequently introduced a larger format in 1983 (no. 60), which still survives, in keeping with his aims of a more flexible layout.

Brown saw the heavier paper and larger format as more than simply stylistic design alterations.

> There was something about the quality of the editorial, about a certain sort of credibility and generosity that I think needed to be conveyed. And it was not just the size that I spent a lot of time on but I spent a lot of time on the paper. It's got to feel right when you hold it so that it doesn't fold up and feel like a woman's magazine. So, that's why we went to uncoated paper because it bulks out more and feels more substantial.[14]

It was the work of David King that caused the most controversy. While the most damning criticism recalled by Bruce Brown was that he had turned the magazine into 'something like *Vogue*', King's imposition of bold bands of colour, and neo-constructivist graphic styling, was not universally admired.[15] The design was seen as overshadowing the work, though, in fact, the work of the 1980s was no longer the elitist, painstaking one-off of *The Craftsman's Art* exhibition. King actually confessed to having no interest in the crafts and saw his role as an agitator who could revive and reorganise what he saw as the sleepy, hidebound world of a government-supported publication. Significantly, he referred to the magazine unsentimentally as a 'product'.[16]

9.1 *Crafts* magazine cover, Issue 36, 1979: Box, silver and copper by Michael Rowe photographed by David Cripps.

In order to act as a gallery-without-walls, *Crafts* pursued the most rigorous quality of presentation in its photography. Photographers such as Ron Bagley and David Cripps created inspired images for objects that sometimes did not live up to their glamour. Cripps, employed at *Design* as one of its graphic designers, already owned a collection of early twentieth-century ceramics. His contribution was highly influential, producing thirty-five out of the first fifty covers (Figure 9.1). His use of lighting and obsession with detail is a triumph in the art of describing, inducting readers in how to look at craft objects. Commenting on his cover for no. 36, 1979, Cripps revealed his subtle methods:

> It's still the aesthetic object, Michael Rowe with his distorted perspectives … and I altered the horizon line, as a comment about the thing … A lot of it they didn't notice and I'm glad. It wasn't meant to overpower. It's not supposed to interfere with the object; it's meant to add to it.[17]

In contrast, David King's iconoclastic methods revealed his exasperation with the muted, wry asceticism of the earlier approaches. No longer relying mainly on one photographer, and using images for his own stylistic ends, King declared:

> If a photograph is worth using, then you use it big, and in fact big isn't even big enough. You crop it in; you make it even bigger, as big as possible. And then you put junior photographs next door to it, which makes it look even bigger. And you have sort of close-ups and long-shots. You break up the pages with multi-photo pages.[18]

(See Figure 9.2.)

Bruce Brown saw the way in which the conflicting demands within *Crafts* had reached a crisis point by 1981.

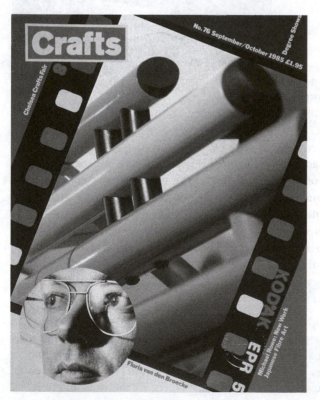

9.2 *Crafts* magazine cover, Issue 76, 1985: Detail of 'S:E:T: T:L:E BCC '85' by Floris van den Broecke photographed by Philip Sayer.

In my view the magazine is advertising; in a nice sense it's advertising products. But to have it jumbled up with real advertising, which actually was quite tacky, was really difficult ... I just thought the language was so confused. I simply said we needed to distinguish between the two languages. The language of the editorial, which because of the nature of the editorial is confused with the language of the advertising. And we have to make it clear to the readers, which is which.[19]

The magazine was primarily the site for the consumption and fetishisation of handmade objects but the conflicting languages in the magazine are evidence of the constant struggle to police the border between 'new' Craft Council approved work and that of the amateur.

Written – *Crafts*

The historical subjects included in the early issues, reveal which traditions were deemed relevant to contemporary practice and could act as legitimators of the new craft.[20] Although the Arts and Crafts Movement stood as an *ur*-precedent of the artist-crafts, the fluctuation between 'designer-craftsperson' and 'artist-craftsman' in the early 1980s made possible a new set of historical precedents.

In keeping with the broad remit of the early issues, the Fulham Pottery in the seventeenth century was the first historical subject broached by the magazine.[21] However, a year later, in 1975 the perceptive critic and writer John Houston began a series on 'the history of the schism between art and craft', an ideological debate at the heart of contemporary craft practice. Houston traced many of the myths of the artist to the Italian Renaissance as well as 'the concept of art as an intellectual experiment'[22] underlining the ruptures between art and craft of the time. In his final article on the Bauhaus' commitment to craft practices he quoted Walter Gropius.

Only work, which is the product of an inner compulsion, can have spiritual meaning. Mechanized work is lifeless, proper only to the lifeless machine ... The solution depends on a change in the individual's attitude towards his work.[23]

This could be seen to perfectly echo the sentiments of both the Craft Council's mission and that of its constituency.

The publication of Christopher Frayling and Helen Snowdon's 'Craft

Perspectives I–V' in the 'Comment' section of the magazine highlighted its intellectual potential without compromising the need to be accessible to a broad range of readers.[24] Nevertheless, anxieties at the Crafts Council that the magazine was sometimes 'a bit highbrow' ultimately diverted academic debate into other publications such as *The Journal of Design History*.[25]

In *The Fashion System* (1985) Roland Barthes asked the key question: what happens when 'an object is converted into language'?[26] *Crafts* and craft objects occupy a comparable dynamic space to that presented in Barthes' study: the technological, the iconic and the verbal. Just as fashion is 'directed towards a set of collective representations', so *Crafts* functioned to circulate 'broadly as *meaning*'.[27] The magazine provided a forum for articulating contesting definitions of craft practice. Frayling's and Snowdon's early 1980s research demonstrated that craftspeople:

> agreed that craft activity represents a type of knowledge the effectiveness of which can be demonstrated rather than articulated in a verbal way.[28]

The ceramicist Elizabeth Fritsch was one of the early contributors who proved that practitioners could write eloquently about their practice. Reviewing an exhibition by Glenys Barton, she writes,

> Glenys Barton explores the precision and the machine tooled extremes of the ceramic medium more intensely perhaps than any other artist … [she] takes great pains to grind and polish [the slabs] thus asserting high standards of accuracy and meticulousness of finish. Thus she dictates a deliberate and extreme coldness.[29]

The formalist language of mid-century modernism proved particularly popular with ceramicists such as Jacqueline Poncelet.

> I'm working very hard on the edges. You see, I've always asked people to ignore the edges of my pots … With these recent pots, I felt I was making a breakthrough because the edges are not denied.[30]

Blind to the masculine bias of modernism, and subscribing to the ideology of aesthetic autonomy, *Crafts* attempted to maintain a disinterestedness that might ally the works with the dominant culture of the fine arts.

The duality of the artist-craftsperson indicated the desire to link together the intellectual attainment of the fine arts with the technical virtuosity associated with craftsmanship. Consequently, there was, from the very beginning, what the first editor, Marigold Coleman, called 'the ongoing question' of who the magazine was for. Coleman's editorship focused on mapping the terrain and its constituents. Nine features in the second issue of 1973 were described in the subheadings as: 'interviews', 'visits', 'meetings'. By the 1980s, this had become writers who 'comment', 'review', 'explain', 'argue' (nos 71, 1984 and 72, 1985). Coleman observed of her writers that they did not,

> Fit glibly into any category – craftsman, writer, teacher, whatever. They are simply people unafraid to say what they feel, and able to feel directly, innocently, if you like, uncluttered by old phobias and preconceptions at the moment of seeing.[31]

The emphasis on promoting a sense of craft as expressive and personal which offers something 'more than function' was crucial.

> The emotive language of feeling had its roots in the sensual delight of the decorative, a concept central to much craft appreciation. Nevertheless, process was also represented by articles such as 'Lutes and Citerns: Basic principles for those thinking of making their own instruments'.[32]

The amount of technical information necessary was a matter of some unease, in other words, should *Crafts* become a kind of how-to-do-it magazine.[33]

John Hawkins' resolution to this was to let the caption take up the burden of technical information. Although the magazine seemed to have a constituency and a purpose, the brief was complex. As Coleman observed:

> I was asked to do a magazine for practitioners. But, in some ways who were the practitioners? A ceramicist, a jeweller, a textile maker. They have areas in common but they have their own specialities so there is no [one] practitioner … There was also the remit of the CAC – to increase the audience of the crafts.[34]

The first issue resolved the dilemma by announcing: '*Crafts* is a magazine for the craftsman and all those interested in his work'.

Coleman's enthusiasm coupled with the pioneering spirit at the

CAC, meant that the magazine started with vision and energy. Contradictions were embraced. 'So there was a brilliant balancing act you kept by keeping them all together and getting a little bit of their richness acceptable to everyone.'[35] Initially, the editor did much of the writing 'in a straightforward way, not pretending that I knew anything'. Partly this was also because it was difficult to 'find professional journalists who knew very much about what we were trying to do and sometimes they were disasters when one tried to use them. So I started out by using craftspeople'.[36]

Martina Margetts, who was to follow Coleman as the first full-time editor in 1979 later commissioned professional writers and journalists. Like Coleman, Margetts' initial knowledge of the crafts was sketchy but she pointed out that it was a small field and journalists 'know very quickly what's what'.[37] Margetts nurtured a group of writers who went on to become prominent critics and journalists: Deyan Sudjic, Stephen Bayley, Tanya Harrod and Peter Dormer.[38]

Of all the writers, Peter Fuller stands out as one of *Crafts'* most provocative and thoughtful commentators. Fuller was committed to a Ruskinian vision of the applied arts at odds with the prevailing neo-avant-gardism of the so-called 'Krazy Kat' generation. The ceramicist and writer Alison Britton, in an article describing the various influences on her contemporaries' work had used this term – a reference to the artist Eduardo Paolozzi's eclectic collection of pop ephemera.[39] Fuller believed such work was useless, unattractive and uninteresting:

> Born out of the Late Modernist dogmas that novelty, rejection of tradition and uninhibited 'questioning of the medium' are essential, indeed sole criteria of value.[40]

His belief that the crafts should provide a 'shared symbolic order' was more in tune with vernacular traditions espoused by potters such as Michael Cardew and Bernard Leach.

Counterculture to subculture

Craftwork's appeal as unalienated labour, was and remains an important characteristic. An early article, 'A Craft Community' described the Dove Centre of Creativity in Somerset.[41] Its director wished for 'the proverbial cottage in the country' where he and his family and others could do something 'personal and expressive'. Students would learn 'by watching', and there would be a breakdown of class barriers. The food was bought in bulk and cooked by a vegetarian chef. It typified what Victor Margrie referred to as 'the brown bread and sandals Seventies period' the drop-out counterculture moment.[42]

> Brown stoneware pottery signified counter cultural values, and in an emerging semiotically aware culture, craft objects played a key role as cultural markers of such otherness.

Although political activism accounted for a high proportion of counter-cultural values, the research of Frank Musgrove revealed that art students at Hornsey College of Art in 1968 spurned conventional success and security, preferring the freedom of self-employment.[43] By 1979, however, the furniture maker David Field announced that 'the crafts are not for opting out'.[44] The shift can be detected in the marginalisation of the community workshops to the rise of urban studios such as 401½ in Wandsworth (no. 41), and the Glasshouse in Covent Garden. Counter-culture ruralism was transforming into environmentalism:

> Events at Chernobyl underline the need for nations to reconsider their priorities … not in a nostalgic or sixties drop-out vein but as reflection of contemporary attitudes. The craftspeople featured indicate a positive commitment to making work a contribution to, and expression of, a particular quality of life in which our natural and human resources are sympathetically balanced. [These] craftspeople offer ironic commentaries on our materialistic culture and the function and meaning of possessions.[45]

If the early craft movement is marked by a tendency to work outside the rat race of conventional manufacturing, by the mid-1980s collaborations with industry were presented as ideal practice, reinforcing the crafts' contribution to new developments in technology. The pressures of commercial viability, the relevance of the crafts in an industrial economy meant that the Crafts Council and the magazine needed to foreground a feasible role for the crafts in the economic health of the country, while not abandoning the ideals of unalienated labour.

Craft, art, design: the eternal triangle

The emancipation of the craft object from its pedestal as 'art' was achieved in the mid-1980s with the increasing prominence of furniture as well as a shift in terminology from 'the artist-craftsman' to the 'designer-craftsperson'. However, Erik de Graaff's 'Body Tools' were 'scrutinised' by the future director of the Design Museum, Stephen Bayley, who pointed out, notions of the chair as 'art' were not new but the potential blind alley of de Graaff's experiments in seating hovered over many craft practices.

> So far, not being interested in selling his designs … de Graaff has not had the opportunity to test the public's response to his ideas about furniture. This form of solipsism has been associated with fine artists ever since the Romantics blasted a causeway between art and the public, and if de Graaff's chairs do little to advance the business of having nice things to sit on, by being striking objects with ideological sophistication, he reaffirms the status of art in the artist-craftsman's role.[46]

This is a tendency that Deyan Sudjic writing in 1982 identified as the difference between 'writing a diary in code and writing a novel'.[47]

Discussion about the significance of the craft object as art, as design, and the role of craftsmanship formed the focus of the critical debate. However, unlike fine art and design with their secured vocabulary and rules of practice, new craft attempted to establish its autonomy while at the same time drawing on the practices and discourses of fine art and design. It was in this sense that autonomy eluded the crafts even at the level of individual practices, which reproduced the paradox at a local level highlighted in the case of ceramics/pottery. Although ceramics was the most popular craft practised, the CAC had been conscious that *Ceramic Review* was already catering for that market.[48] Given that publications on craft matters were few, competition would have been counterproductive.[49] In the first twenty issues, only fifteen articles featured ceramics while there were twenty-three on textiles, the second most popular practice, including a whole issue 'mainly about clothes' (no. 13, 1975). In the review sections the significance of pottery becomes clear: thirty ceramic exhibitions as against eighteen textile events. This figure does not include mixed shows where pottery usually predominated.

Ceramics provided exemplary evidence for the continuing debate between the traditionalists and the newcomers. Skill became the core argument in studio ceramics, to be repeated within all craft practices. The art/craft divide had been broached in 'Sculptures in Limbo' (no. 33) where Glenys Barton, Barry Flanagan and Gordon Baldwin discussed the problem of categorisation. The last word was given to the painter Helen Wilks who was keen to preserve the distinctions, suggesting that the artist 'is unable to 'foretell the end' of his creative adventure, unlike the craftsman whose work is bound not only by material and technique but the 'form and function of his object'.[50] Barton countered this by pointing to the teaching in art colleges where sculpture students were introduced to concepts such as space, form, and surface while ceramic students had to 'reach ideas through working with the material'.[51]

*Craft*speople

Just as the proportion of women practitioners in the crafts was high, the editors of *Crafts* have all been and continue to be women: Marigold Coleman (1973–79), Martina Margetts (1979–87), Pamela Johnson (1987–88), and Geraldine Rudge (1988–2006). Nevertheless, the emergence of the term 'craftspeople' seems almost unbearably delayed. *Crafts* did not include any feminist reference until 1982 when 'Domestic Bliss' by Penina Barnett (no. 53) explored the terms: art, artist, male, craft, craftsman, female. Textiles in the magazine, a practice dominated by women, reinforced the stereotypical conjunction of women and craft. For instance, an article on embroiderer Lucy Goffin enthused:

> Her name could easily belong to a Beatrix Potter character. [Her] stitching would do justice to the Tailor of Gloucester … She is remarkably modest … Obviously the question of having to put a price on anything is painful. She would rather give things away, make them especially for her dear friends.[52]

Such essentialism could not be sustained given the shift in feminist sensibility. The rise of the 'new' art history, especially the work of Griselda Pollock and Rozika Parker, which impacted specifically on the history of textiles and needlework, nevertheless, was never incorporated into the magazine's remit.[53]

The increasing professionalism of craftspeople was abetted by the Setting-up Grants introduced by the Crafts Council in 1975. Bursaries, fellowships and awards were continuously advertised in the magazine.

The introduction of art history and complimentary studies into the art school's teaching programme as a result of the 1960s Coldstream Reports 'brought an increasingly academic orientation' to the work of art-school students.[54] It is arguable that an academic orientation fostered conceptual approaches that widened the gap between industry and the art schools. Summarising the discussion at the Design and Industries Association seminar held at the Royal College of Art in June 1977, *Crafts* reported that students in the late 1970s were felt to be 'just not tough enough with industry or not sufficiently interested in working for industry'.[55] By 1984 however, students had evolved into 'High Flyers' [no. 70] who, alongside continuing aims to set up workshops for one-offs '... wish to collaborate with architects, interior and theatre designers, and manufacturers'.[56]

Degree shows were evaluated by the work of individual students whose work was shown in the pages of the magazine. By the mid-1980s, portraits of students began to be included alongside the work. 'Art students had to shine as personalities because of the enormous uncertainties.'[57] In 1987, the designer Tom Dixon stared moodily out of the front cover photographed by Patrick Shanahan. Only the magazine's logo gives an indication that the photograph signifies 'craft'. Pictured during his metal salvage phase, the image attempted to echo the sub-cultural glamour to be found in magazines such *The Face* and *I-D* (Figure 9.3).

This portrayal of celebrity designer-makers could not have been further from Yanagi's impossible vision of the 'unknown craftsman'.[58] 'The virtue of folkcrafts is that one feels no obtruding personality in them. The things shines, not the maker.'[59]

Sub-culture as the construction of a style in a gesture of defiance or contempt also played a part in the construction of the makers featured in the 1980s.[60] The anomalous position of the crafts as a 'sanctioned' alternative, supported by the official body of the Crafts Council and represented in the collection of the Victoria & Albert Museum, meant that it sought its defiance in stylistic subversions of the Arts and Crafts ideal of fine workmanship. Metal 'bashing' can be seen as the stylistic

9.3 *Crafts* magazine cover, Issue 87, 1987. Tom Dixon photographed by Patrick Shanahan.

action of defiance to a hegemony of preciousness. 'The New Spirit in Craft and Design' exhibition of 1987 presented what the curator and craft writer, Ralph Turner described as, 'Youth's reaction against everything that [was] thought normal, tasteful, safe, middle-aged or middle-class',[61] Nevertheless, Margetts pinpointed the essential qualities which she felt the magazine should uphold:

> I wouldn't like to see the crafts world becoming quite so blatantly personality orientated. I really think it is a wonderful thing if the work can come first … And there is a danger … if you're putting people on the cover that you're really saying that the people are … everything.[62]

Conclusion

Crafts magazine was a key mechanism in the construction and dissemination of the craft system, established by 'written-craft' and 'image-craft'.
The consumption of the text, either as information under the editorship
of Marigold Coleman, or as polemic under the editorship of Martina
Margetts, mapped the structural shifts within craft, art and design during
the period 1971–87. At each stage, the fetishised consumption of craft
objects was sustained and reinforced by its images:

> Our relationship with goods is almost entirely one of consumption ...
> [goods] might be divided into those we possess and those we encounter
> but do not possess ...
>
> Goods not possessed tend to fall into two categories; first those
> we encounter as material forms ... and secondly, goods we do not
> experience directly, but which appear to us through the media.[63]

The lack of engagement with political and social issues, and the commitment to an elitist definition of craft, could be seen to be confirmed in
Crafts incarnation as a magazine of 'the decorative and applied arts', the
subtitle it acquired in 1988. Incorporating work from fine art ceramics
to fashion, the symbolic capital of craft became diluted. Having given up
its struggle for legitimacy, craft products and producers now appear in
a variety of other publications, such *Blueprint, World of Interiors*, and/or
specialist journals such as *Ceramic Review*.

In a system of cultural production where autonomy is still a measure
of visibility and success craft as represented in the magazine was never
able to 'define its own criteria for the production and evaluation of its
products',[64] though not through lack of trying. The attempt to *define*
craft was inevitably doomed, given that from its inception the magazine
sought to incorporate a diversity of producers whose struggle for status
or for control of the field, was overshadowed by the dominant fields of
fine art and design.[65]

Craft discourse has been dominated by the art/craft debate, which is
now seen as outmoded.[66] Never entirely resolved, it continues to haunt
craft's identity. Bourdieu's observation that '*the struggle itself* creates the
history of the field,'[67] may therefore provide a way to reconsider the
history and representation of *Crafts* for crafts' sake.

Notes

1 Hereafter called the CAC.

2 Crafts Council, *Report 1982–1985* (London: Crafts Council, 1985), p.3.

3 For a discussion of the term 'craft' see P.Greenhalgh, 'The History of Craft' in P.Dormer (ed.), *The Culture of Craft* (Manchester: Manchester University Press, 1997).

4 P.Bourdieu, *Distinction: A Social Critique of the Judgement of Taste* (London: Routledge & Kegan Paul, 1984), p.481. The CAC became the Crafts Council and received its Royal Charter in 1974.

5 Crafts Advisory Committee, *The Work of the Crafts Advisory Committee: Report 1977–1980* (London: Crafts Council, 1980).

6 'Introduction', *Crafts*, 1 (March 1973), p.22.

7 See M.Featherstone, *Consumer Culture and Postmodernism* (London: Sage Publications, 1991), p.67.

8 P.Bourdieu, *The Field of Cultural Production* (Cambridge: Polity Press, 1933), p.75.

9 Joint interview (9 January 1991) with Marigold Coleman, editor, *Crafts*, 1 (March 1973) to *Crafts*, 36 (March/April 1979), and Victor Margrie, Secretary of the CAC, then Director of the Crafts Council until 1984, p.21. Full transcript of this and all other interviews quoted can be read in Linda Sandino, *Crafts for Crafts Sake: From Counterculture to Subculture*, MA thesis, V&A/RCA, 1991.

10 Interview (7 March 1991) with Martina Margetts, editor, *Crafts*, 36 (January/February 1979) to *Crafts*, 89 (May/June 1987).

11 See R.Barthes, *The Fashion System* (Berkeley: University of California Press, 1985), p.244, where Barthes discusses the denotation of luxury and popular fashion magazines. See also P.Jobling, *Fashion Spreads: Word and Image in Fashion Photography since 1980* (Oxford: Berg, 1999).

12 Interview (13 March 1991) with David King, art director, *Crafts*, 69 (July/August 1984) to *Crafts*, 91 (March/April 1988), p.7.

13 See Interview with B.Brown, p.7.

14 Ibid.

15 Interview with M.Margetts, pp.12–15.

16 Interview with David King, p.3.

17 Interview (13 February 1991) with David Cripps, photographer, p.5.

18 Interview with D.King, p.10.

19 Interview with B. Brown, p. 3.

20 See E. Hobsbawm and T. Ranger, *The Invention of Tradition* (Cambridge: Cambridge University Press, 1983).

21 *Crafts*, 9 (July/August 1974).

22 J. Houston, 'Ghiberti and the Great Schism', *Crafts*, 12 (Jan./Feb. 1975), p. 30.

23 J. Houston, 'The Bauhaus and the Crafts', *Crafts*, 14 (May/June 1975), p. 14.

24 C. Frayling and H. Snowdon, 'The Myth of the Happy Artisan', *Crafts*, 54 (Jan./Feb. 1982), pp. 16–17: 'Crafts With or Without Art', *Crafts*, 55 (May/April), pp. 24–25: 'Skill a Word to Start an Argument With', *Crafts*, 56 (May/June), pp. 19–21: 'Crafts in the Marketplace', *Crafts*, 57 (July/Aug.), pp. 15–17: 'Nostalgia Ain't What it Used to Be', *Crafts*, 59 (Nov./Dec.), pp. 12–13.

25 See, for example, *The Journal of Design History*, vol. 2, Issues 2–3 (1989), and vol. 11, Issue 1 (1998).

26 R. Barthes, *The Fashion System* (Berkeley: University of California Press) 1990, p. 12.

27 Ibid., p .9.

28 C. Frayling and H. Snowdon, *Crafts*, 56 (May/June 1982), p. 19.

29 *Crafts*, 12 (Jan./Feb.1975), p. 48.

30 *Crafts*, 50 (May/June1981), p. 24.

31 *Crafts*, 35 (Nov./Dec. 1978), p. 1.

32 *Crafts*, 3 (July/August 1973), pp. 20–23.

33 See interview with D. Cripps, p. 16.

34 See interview with M. Coleman and V. Margrie, p. 5.

35 Ibid., p. 7.

36 Ibid., p. 11.

37 Interview with M. Margetts, p. 8.

38 Deyan Sudjic became editor of *Blueprint*, Stephen Bayley, Director of the Boilerhouse at the V&A, Tanya Harrod and Peter Dormer, went on to write extensively about the crafts.

39 A. Britton, 'Sevres with Krazy Kat', *Crafts*, 61 (March/April 1983), pp. 18–23.

40 P. Fuller, 'The Proper Work of the Potter', in *Images of God: the Consolation of Lost Illusions* (London: The Hogarth Press, 1985). See also his review of the contemporary ceramics exhibition 'Fast Forward' in *Crafts*, 75 (July/August), 1985, pp. 47–48.

41 A. Horrocks, 'A Craft Community', *Crafts*, 1 (March 1973), pp. 13–15.

42 Interview V. Margrie (and M. Coleman), p. 16.

43 F. Musgrove. *Ecstasy and Holiness: Counter Culture and the Open Society* (London: Methuen, 1974), p. 6.

44 *Crafts*, 39 (July/August 1979), p. 9.

45 *Crafts*, 81 (July/August 1986), p. 2.

46 S. Bayley, 'Body Tools'. *Crafts*, 45 (July/August 1980), pp. 28–9.

47 D. Sudjic, 'Comment: Backwoods or Forwards', *Crafts*, 56 (May/June 1982), p. 16.

48 A. Bruce and P. Filmer, *Working in the Crafts* (London: Crafts Council, 1983).

49 Interview with M. Coleman and V. Margrie, p. 16.

50 'Sculptures in Limbo'. *Crafts*, 33 (July/August 1978), p. 34.

51 Ibid.

52 *Crafts*, 6 (January/February 1974), p. 34.

53 See, for example: R. Parker and G. Pollock, *Old Mistresses: Women, Art and Ideology* (London: Routledge, Kegan Paul, 1981); R. Parker, *The Subversive Stitch: Embroidery and the Making of the Feminine* (London: The Women's Press, 1984).

54 A. Bruce and P. Filmer, *Working in the Crafts* (London: Crafts Council, 1983), p. 88.

55 *Crafts*, 28 (September/October 1977), p. 11.

56 *Crafts*, 70 (September/October 1984), p. 45.

57 Ibid.

58 'In terms of total responses, the emergent picture was that "designer" was the most popular descriptor followed by "maker", "artist" and "designer-maker". The use of "craftsman", "designer-craftsman" and "artist-craftsman" lagged far behind.' In C. Ashwin, A. Channon, J. Darracott, *Education for the Crafts: A Study of the Education and Training of Craftspeople in England and Wales* (London: Crafts Council, Middlesex Polytechnic, 1988), p. 65.

59 S. Yanagi, 'The Unknown Craftsman', *Crafts*, 2 (March 1973), pp. 43–44.

60 For a pertinent discussion of sub-culture see D. Hebdige, *Subculture: The Meaning of Style* (London: Routledge, 1979).

61 Quoted in T. Harrod, *The Crafts in Britain in the Twentieth Century* (London: Yale University Press, 1999), p. 442.

62 Interview M. Margetts, p. 17.

63 D. Miller, *Material Culture and Mass Consumption* (Oxford: Basil Blackwell,

1987), p. 53.

64 P. Bourdieu, *The Field of Cultural Production* (Cambridge: Polity Press, 1993), p. 115.

65 See A. Jackson 'Against the Autonomy of the Craft Object', in *Obscure Objects of Desire: Reviewing the Crafts in the Twentieth Century*, conference papers, University of East Anglia (ed.) T. Harrod (London: Crafts Council), 1997, pp. 284–291. Jackson takes issue with the Crafts Council's espousal of what he terms 'high' craft.

66 P. Greenhalgh (ed.), 'Introduction: Craft in a Changing World', in *The Persistence of Craft: The Applied Arts Today* (London: A & C Black, 2003).

67 Bourdieu, *'The Field of Cultural Production*, p. 106.

Index